The Lectionary
2023

First published in Great Britain in 2022

Society for Promoting Christian Knowledge
36 Causton Street
London SW1P 4ST
www.spck.org.uk

British Library Cataloguing-in-Publication Data
A catalogue record for this book is available from the British Library

ISBN 978-0-281-08669-6
ISBN 978-0-281-08670-2 (spiral-bound)

1 3 5 7 9 10 8 6 4 2

Designed by Colin Hall, Refined Practice
Typeset by Fakenham Prepress Solutions, Fakenham, Norfolk NR21 8NL
Printed in Great Britain by Ashford Colour Press

Produced on paper from sustainable forests

CONTENTS

UNDERSTANDING THE LECTIONARY

Common Worship on left-hand page

June 2023		Sunday Principal Service Weekday Eucharist	Third Service Morning Prayer	Common Worship Second Service Evening Prayer
17 Saturday	*Samuel and Henrietta Barnett, Social Reformers, 1913 and 1936*			
G		2 Cor. 5. 14–end Ps. 103. 1–12 Matt. 5. 33–37	Ps. 41; *42*; 43 2 Chron. 36. 11–end Rom. 8. 31–end	Ps. 45; *46* Josh. 24. 29–end Luke 12. 49–end *ct*
18 Sunday	**THE SECOND SUNDAY AFTER TRINITY (Proper 6)**			
G	*Track 1* Gen. 18. 1–15 [21. 1–7] Ps. 116. 1, 10–17 (or 116. 9–17) Rom. 5. 1–8 Matt. 9.35 – 10.8 [9–23]	*Track 2* Exod. 19. 2–8a Ps. 100 Rom. 5. 1–8 Matt. 9.35 – 10.8 [9–23]	Ps. 45 Deut. 10.12 – 11.1 Acts 23. 12–end	Ps. [42]; 43 1 Sam. 21. 1–15 Luke 11. 14–28
19 Monday	*Sundar Singh of India, Sadhu (holy man), Evangelist, Teacher, 1929*			
G **DEL 11**		2 Cor. 6. 1–10 Ps. 98 Matt. 5. 38–42	Ps. 44 Ezra ch. 1 Rom. 9. 1–18	Ps. *47*; 49 Judg. ch. 2 Luke 13. 1–9

Column 1
- Date
- **Colour:** An upper-case letter indicates the liturgical colour of the day. A lower-case second colour indicates the colour for a Lesser Festival while the upper-case letter indicates the continuing seasonal colour.
- **DEL:** Week number of Daily Eucharistic Lectionary.

Column 2
- Name of the Principal Holy Day, Sunday, Festival or Lesser Festival;
- a note of other Commemorations for mention in prayers;
- any general note that applies to the whole *Common Worship* provision for the day;
- one of the options where there are two options for readings at the Eucharist or Principal Service.

Readings: Readings occur in this column only in two circumstances.

1. **On Sundays after Trinity** where there are two 'tracks' for the Principal Service readings (where there is a choice of first reading and psalm, but the second reading and Gospel are the same in both tracks), Track I appears in this column.

2. **On Lesser Festivals throughout the year** where there are readings for that festival that are alternative to the semi-continuous Daily Eucharistic Lectionary, these also appear in this column.

Column 3
On Principal Feasts, **Principal Holy Days, Sundays and Festivals** this gives the Principal Service Lectionary, intended for use at the main service of the day (in most churches the mid-morning service), whether or not it is a Eucharist.

On other weekdays this gives the Daily Eucharistic Lectionary for those wanting a semi-continuous pattern of readings and a psalm for Holy Communion. It is most useful in a church where there is a daily celebration and a core community that worships together day by day, though its use is not restricted to that.

On Sundays after Trinity where there are two 'tracks' for the Principal Service readings (where there is a choice of first reading and psalm, but the second reading and Gospel are the same in both tracks), Track 2 appears in this column.

Column 4
On Principal Feasts, **Principal Holy Days, Sundays and Festivals** this gives the Third Service Lectionary. Many churches will have no need of it, for it comes into use only if the Principal and Second Service Lectionaries have been used. Its most likely use is at Morning Prayer (when this is not the Principal Service). Where psalms are recommended for use in the morning, these also appear in this column.

On other weekdays this provides the psalmody and readings for Morning **Prayer.** Where two or more psalms are appointed, the psalm in bold italic may be used as the only psalm. Psalms printed in round brackets ( ) may be omitted if they are used as an opening canticle at Morning Prayer. Where † is printed after the psalm number, the psalm may be shortened if desired. For those wishing to follow the Ordinary Time psalm cycle throughout the year (except for the period between 19 December and the Epiphany and from the Monday of Holy Week to the Saturday of Easter Week), this is printed as an alternative to the seasonal provision.

Column 5
On Principal Feasts, Principal Holy Days, Sundays and Festivals this gives the Second Service Lectionary, intended for use when a second set of readings is required. Its most likely use is in the evening, when the Principal Service Lectionary has been used in the morning. Sometimes it might be used at an evening Eucharist. Where the second reading is not a Gospel reading, an alternative to meet this need is provided. Where psalms are recommended for use in the evening, these also appear in this column.

On other weekdays this provides the psalmody and readings for Evening Prayer. Where two or more psalms are provided, the psalm in bold italic may be used as the only psalm. Psalms printed in round brackets ( ) may be omitted if they are used as an opening canticle at Evening Prayer. Where † is printed after the psalm number, the psalm may be shortened if desired. For those wishing to follow the Ordinary Time psalm cycle throughout the year (except for the period between 19 December and the Epiphany and from the Monday of Holy Week to the Saturday of Easter Week), this is printed as an alternative to the seasonal provision.

Book of Common Prayer

June 2023

	Calendar and Holy Communion	Morning Prayer	Evening Prayer	NOTES
	Alban, first Martyr of Britain, c. 250			
Gr	Com. Martyr	2 Chron. 36. 11–end Rom. 8. 31–end	Josh. 24. 29–end Luke 12. 49–end	
			ct	
	THE SECOND SUNDAY AFTER TRINITY			
G	Gen. 12. 1–4 Ps. 120 1 John 3. 13–end Luke 14. 16–24	Ps. 45 Deut. 10.12 – 11.1 Acts 23. 12–end	Ps. [42]; 43 1 Sam. 21. 1–15 Luke 11. 14–28	
G		Ezra ch. 1 Rom. 9. 1–18	Judg. ch. 2 Luke 13. 1–9	

Column 6	Column 7	Column 8	Column 9	Column 10
Liturgical colour (*see column 1*).	• The name of the Principal Holy Day, Sunday, Festival or Lesser Festival; • any general note that applies to the whole Prayer Book provision for the day and an indication of points at which users may wish to draw on *Common Worship* material on the opposite page where the BCP has no provision; • the Lectionary for the Eucharist on any day for which provision is made.	This provides the readings for Morning Prayer, together with psalm provision where it varies from the BCP monthly cycle.	This provides the readings for Evening Prayer, together with psalm provision where it varies from the BCP monthly cycle. A letter to indicate liturgical colour in this column indicates a change of colour for Evening Prayer. The symbol in bold lower case, **ct**, indicates that the Collect at Evening Prayer should be that of the following day. This also applies to column 5.	Space for notes.

ABBREVIATIONS OF BOOKS OF THE BIBLE

Old Testament

Gen. (Genesis)	Kings	Song of Sol. (Song of Solomon)	Obad. (Obadiah)
Exod. (Exodus)	Chron. (Chronicles)	Isa. (Isaiah)	Jonah
Lev. (Leviticus)	Ezra	Jer. (Jeremiah)	Mic. (Micah)
Num. (Numbers)	Neh. (Nehemiah)	Lam. (Lamentations)	Nahum
Deut. (Deuteronomy)	Esth. (Esther)	Ezek. (Ezekiel)	Hab. (Habakkuk)
Josh. (Joshua)	Job	Dan. (Daniel)	Zeph. (Zephaniah)
Judg. (Judges)	Ps. (Psalms)	Hos. (Hosea)	Hag. (Haggai)
Ruth	Prov. (Proverbs)	Joel	Zech. (Zechariah)
Sam. (Samuel)	Eccles. (Ecclesiastes)	Amos	Mal. (Malachi)

Apocrypha

Esd. (Esdras)	Wisd. (Wisdom of Solomon)	Song of the Three (Song of the Three Children)	Prayer of Manasseh
Tob. (Tobit)	Ecclus. (Ecclesiasticus)	Susanna (The History of Susanna)	Macc. (Maccabees)
Judith	Baruch		

New Testament

Matt. (Matthew)	Cor. (Corinthians)	Tim. (Timothy)	John (letters of John)
Mark	Gal. (Galatians)	Titus	Jude
Luke	Eph. (Ephesians)	Philem. (Philemon)	Rev. (Revelation)
John	Phil. (Philippians)	Heb. (Hebrews)	
Acts (Acts of the Apostles)	Col. (Colossians)	James	
Rom. (Romans)	Thess. (Thessalonians)	Pet. (Peter)	

MAKING CHOICES IN COMMON WORSHIP

Common Worship makes provision for a variety of pastoral and liturgical circumstances. It needs to, for it has to serve some church communities where Morning Prayer, Holy Communion and Evening Prayer are all celebrated every day, and yet be useful also in a church with only one service a week, and that service varying in form and time from week to week.

At the beginning of the year, some decisions in principle need to be taken.

In relation to the Calendar, whether to keep The Epiphany on Friday 6 January or on Sunday 8 January, whether to keep The Presentation of Christ (Candlemas) on Thursday 2 February or on Sunday 29 January, and whether to keep the Feast of All Saints on Wednesday 1 November or on Sunday 5 November.

In relation to the Lectionary, the initial choices every year to decide in relation to Sundays are:

- which of the services on a Principal Feast, Principal Holy Day, Sunday or Festival constitutes the 'Principal Service'; then use the Principal Service Lectionary (column 3) consistently for that service through the year;

- during the Sundays after Trinity, whether to use Track I of the Principal Service Lectionary (column 2), where the first reading stays over several weeks with one Old Testament book read semi-continuously, or Track 2 (column 3), where the first reading is chosen for its relationship to the Gospel reading of the day;

- which, if any, service on a Principal Feast, Principal Holy Day, Sunday or Festival constitutes the 'Second Service'; then use the Second Service Lectionary (column 5) consistently for that service through the year;

- which, if any, service on a Principal Feast, Principal Holy Day, Sunday or Festival constitutes the 'Third Service'; then use the Third Service Lectionary (column 4) consistently for that service through the year.

And in relation to weekdays:

- whether to use the Daily Eucharistic Lectionary (column 3) consistently for weekday celebrations of Holy Communion (with the exception of Principal Feasts, Principal Holy Days and Festivals) or to make some use of the Lesser Festival provision;

- whether to follow the first psalm provision in column 4 (morning) and column 5 (evening), where psalms during the seasons have a seasonal flavour but in ordinary time follow a sequential pattern; or to follow the alternative provision in the same columns, where psalms follow the sequential pattern throughout the year, except for the period between 19 December and The Epiphany and from the Monday of Holy Week to the Saturday of Easter Week; or to follow the psalm cycle in the Book of Common Prayer, where they are nearly always used 'in course';

- whether to use the Additional Weekday Lectionary (which begins on page 116) for weekday services (other than Holy Communion). It provides a one-year cycle of two readings for each day (except for Sundays, Principal Feasts, Principal Holy Days, Festivals and during Holy Week). Since each of the readings is designed to 'stand alone' (that is, it is complete in itself and will make sense to the worshipper who has not attended on the previous day and who will not be present on the next day), it is intended particularly for use in those churches and cathedrals that attract occasional rather than regular congregations.

The flexibility of Common Worship is intended to enable the church and the minister to find the most helpful provision for them. But once a decision is made, it is advisable to stay with that decision through the year or at the very least through a complete season.

All Bible references (except to the psalms) are to the New Revised Standard Version, Anglicized edition (1995). Those who use other Bible translations should check the verse numbers against the NRSV. References to the psalms are to the Common Worship Psalter.

BOOK OF COMMON PRAYER

A separate Lectionary for the Book of Common Prayer is no longer issued. Provision is made on the right-hand pages of this Lectionary for BCP worship on all Sundays in the year, for the major festivals and for Morning and Evening Prayer. The Epistles and Gospels for Holy Communion are those of 1662, with the additions and variations of 1928, now authorized under the *Common Worship* overall provision. The Old Testament readings and psalms for these services, formerly appended to the Series One Holy Communion service, may be used but are not mandatory with the 1662 order.

Readings for Morning and Evening Prayer, which are the same as those for *Common Worship*, are set out in the BCP section for Sundays and weekdays. The special psalm provision of the BCP is given; however, where the *Common Worship* psalm provision is used, verse numbering may occasionally differ slightly from that in the BCP Psalter, and appropriate adjustment will have to be made (a table of variations in verse numbering can be found at www.churchofengland.org/prayer-and-worship/worship-texts-and-resources/common-worship/daily-prayer/psalter/psalter-verse). Otherwise the Psalter is read in course daily through each month.

The Calendar observes BCP dates when these differ from those of *Common Worship*; for example, St Thomas on 21 December. Additional commemorations in the *Common Worship* Calendar are not included, but those who wish to observe them may use the *Collects and Post Communions in Traditional Language: Lesser Festivals, Common of the Saints, Special Occasions* (Church House Publishing).

The Lectionaries of 1871 and 1922, to be found in many copies of the BCP, are still authorized and may be used, but – with the exception of the psalms and readings for Holy Communion mentioned above – the Additional Alternative Lectionary (1961) is no longer authorized for public worship.

Although those who use the BCP, for private or public worship or both, are free to follow any of the authorized lectionaries, there is much to be said for common usage across the Church of England, so that the same passages are being read by all. It is of course appropriate that BCP readings should be taken from the Authorized or King James Version for harmony of style, with the daily recitation of the BCP Psalter.

The integrity of the BCP as the traditional source of worship in the Church of England is not in any way affected by the use of a common lectionary for the daily offices.

CERTAIN DAYS AND OCCASIONS COMMONLY OBSERVED

Plough Sunday may be observed on 8 January 2023.

The Week of Prayer for Christian Unity may be observed from 18 to 25 January 2023.

Education Sunday may be observed on 10 September 2023.

Rogation Sunday may be observed on 14 May 2023.

The Feast of Dedication is observed on the anniversary of the dedication or consecration of a church, or, when the actual date is unknown, on 1 October 2023. In *Common Worship*, 29 October 2023 is an alternative date.

Ember Days. *Common Worship* encourages the bishop to set the Ember Days in each diocese in the week before the ordinations, whereas in BCP the dates are fixed.

Days of Discipline and Self-Denial in *Common Worship* are the weekdays of Lent and all Fridays in the year, except all Principal Feasts and festivals outside Lent and Fridays between Easter Day and Pentecost. The eves of Principal Feasts are also appropriately kept as days of discipline and self-denial in preparation for the feast.

Days of Fasting and Abstinence according to the BCP are the forty days of Lent, the Ember Days at the four seasons, the three Rogation Days, and all Fridays in the year except Christmas Day. The BCP also orders the observance of the Evens or Vigils before The Nativity of our Lord, The Purification of the Blessed Virgin Mary, The Annunciation of the Blessed Virgin Mary, Easter Day, Ascension Day, Pentecost, and before the following saints' days: Matthias, John the Baptist, Peter, James, Bartholomew, Matthew, Simon and Jude, Andrew, Thomas, and All Saints. (If any of these days falls on Monday, the Vigil is to be kept on the previous Saturday.)

KEY TO LITURGICAL COLOURS

Common Worship suggests appropriate liturgical colours. They are not mandatory, and traditional or local use may be followed.

For a detailed discussion of when colours may be used, see *Common Worship: Services and Prayers for the Church of England* (Church House Publishing), *New Handbook of Pastoral Liturgy* (SPCK) or *A Companion to Common Worship: Volume I* (SPCK).

When a lower-case letter accompanies an upper-case letter, the lower-case letter indicates the liturgical colour appropriate to the Lesser Festival of that day, while the upper-case letter indicates the continuing seasonal colour.

W White
𝖜 Gold or white
R Red
P Purple (may vary from 'Roman purple' to violet, with blue as an alternative; a Lent array of sackcloth may be used in Lent, and rose pink on The Third Sunday of Advent and Fourth Sunday of Lent)
G Green

PRINCIPAL FEASTS, HOLY DAYS AND FESTIVALS

Principal Feasts and other Principal Holy Days (Ash Wednesday, Maundy Thursday, Good Friday) are printed in **LARGE BOLD CAPITALS** in the Lectionary.

There are no longer proper readings relating to the Holy Spirit on the six days after Pentecost. Instead they have been located on the nine days before Pentecost.

When Patronal and Dedication Festivals are kept as Principal Feasts, they may be transferred to the nearest Sunday, unless that day is already either a Principal Feast or The First Sunday of Advent, The Baptism of Christ, The First Sunday of Lent or Palm Sunday.

Festivals are printed in the Lectionary in **SMALL BOLD CAPITALS**.

For each day there is a full liturgical provision for the Holy Communion and for Morning and Evening Prayer. Most holy days that are in the category 'Festival' are provided with an optional First Evening Prayer. Its use is entirely at the discretion of the minister. Where it is used, the liturgical colour for the next day should be used at that First Evening Prayer, and this has been indicated in the provision on the following pages.

LESSER FESTIVALS AND COMMEMORATIONS

Lesser Festivals (printed in **medium-bold roman** typeface) are observed at the level appropriate to a particular church. The readings and psalms for The Common of the Saints are listed on page 10. In addition, there are special readings appropriate to the Festival listed in the first column. The daily psalms and readings at Morning and Evening Prayer are not usually superseded by those for Lesser Festivals, but the readings and psalms for Holy Communion may on occasion be used at Morning or Evening Prayer.

Commemorations are printed in the Lectionary in *italic* typeface. They do not have collect, psalm or readings, but may be observed by mention in prayers of intercession and thanksgiving. For local reasons,

or where there is an established tradition in the wider Church, they may be kept as Lesser Festivals using the appropriate material from The Common of the Saints. Equally, it may be desirable to observe some Lesser Festivals as Commemorations.

If a Lesser Festival or a Commemoration falls on a Principal Feast, Principal Holy Day, Sunday or Festival, it is not normally observed that year, although it may be celebrated, where there is sufficient reason, on the nearest available day. Lesser Festivals and Commemorations which, for this reason, would not be celebrated in 2022–23 are listed on pages 9–10, so that, if desired, they may be mentioned in prayers of intercession and thanksgiving.

LESSER FESTIVALS AND COMMEMORATIONS NOT OBSERVED IN 2022-23

The Lesser Festivals and Commemorations (shown in italics) listed below fall on a Sunday or during Holy Week or Easter Week this year, and are thus not observed in this Lectionary.

COMMON WORSHIP

2022

December
4 *John of Damascus, Monk, Teacher, c. 749*
  Nicholas Ferrar, Deacon, Founder of the Little Gidding Community, 1637

2023

January
22 *Vincent of Saragossa, Deacon, first Martyr of Spain, 304*

March
20 Cuthbert, Bishop of Lindisfarne, Missionary, 687
26 *Harriet Monsell, Founder of the Community of St John the Baptist, Clewer, 1883*

April
9 *Dietrich Bonhoeffer, Lutheran Pastor, Martyr, 1945*
10 William Law, Priest, Spiritual Writer, 1761
   William of Ockham, Friar, Philosopher, Teacher, 1347
11 *George Augustus Selwyn, first Bishop of New Zealand, 1878*
16 *Isabella Gilmore, Deaconess, 1923*
24 *Mellitus, Bishop of London, first Bishop at St Paul's, 624*
   The Seven Martyrs of the Melanesian Brotherhood, Solomon Islands, 2003
30 *Pandita Mary Ramabai, Translator of the Scriptures, 1922*

May
21 *Helena, Protector of the Holy Places, 330*
28 *Lanfranc, Prior of Le Bec, Archbishop of Canterbury, Scholar, 1089*

June
4 *Petroc, Abbot of Padstow, 6th century*
18 *Bernard Mizeki, Apostle of the MaShona, Martyr, 1896*

July
16 *Osmund, Bishop of Salisbury, 1099*
23 *Bridget of Sweden, Abbess of Vadstena, 1373*
30 *William Wilberforce, Social Reformer, Olaudah Equiano and Thomas Clarkson, Anti-Slavery Campaigners, 1833, 1797 and 1846*

August
13 Jeremy Taylor, Bishop of Down and Connor, Teacher, 1667
   Florence Nightingale, Nurse, Social Reformer, 1910
   Octavia Hill, Social Reformer, 1912
20 Bernard, Abbot of Clairvaux, Teacher, 1153
   William and Catherine Booth, Founders of the Salvation Army, 1912 and 1890
27 Monica, Mother of Augustine of Hippo, 387

September
3 Gregory the Great, Bishop of Rome, Teacher, 604
17 Hildegard, Abbess of Bingen, Visionary, 1179

October
1 *Remigius, Bishop of Rheims, Apostle of the Franks, 533*
  Anthony Ashley Cooper, Earl of Shaftesbury, Social Reformer, 1885
15 Teresa of Avila, Teacher, 1582
29 James Hannington, Bishop of Eastern Equatorial Africa, Martyr in Uganda, 1885

November
19 Hilda, Abbess of Whitby, 680
   Mechtild, Béguine of Magdeburg, 1280

December
3 *Francis Xavier, Missionary, Apostle of the Indies, 1552*
17 *Eglantyne Jebb, Social Reformer, Founder of Save the Children, 1928*
31 *John Wyclif, Reformer, 1384*

2023

January
8 Lucian, Priest and Martyr, 290
22 Vincent of Saragossa, Deacon, First Martyr of Spain, 304

February
5 Agatha, Martyr in Sicily, 251

March
12 Gregory the Great, Bishop of Rome, 604

April
3 Richard, Bishop of Chichester, 1253
4 Ambrose, Bishop of Milan, 397

July
2 The Visitation of the Blessed Virgin Mary

September
17 Lambert, Bishop of Maastricht, Martyr, 709

October
1 Remigius, Bishop of Rheims, Apostle of the Franks, 533

December
31 Silvester, Bishop of Rome, 335

THE COMMON OF THE SAINTS

The Blessed Virgin Mary
Genesis 3. 8–15, 20; Isaiah 7. 10–14; Micah 5. 1–4
Psalms 45. 10–17; 113; 131
Acts 1. 12–14; Romans 8. 18–30; Galatians 4. 4–7
Luke 1. 26–38; I. 39–47; John 19. 25–27

Martyrs
2 Chronicles 24. 17–21; Isaiah 43. 1–7;
    Jeremiah 11. 18–20; Wisdom 4. 10–15
Psalms 3; 11; 31. 1–5; 44. 18–24; 126
Romans 8. 35–end; 2 Corinthians 4. 7–15;
    2 Timothy 2. 3–7 [8–13]; Hebrews 11. 32–end;
    1 Peter 4. 12–end; Revelation 12. 10–12a
Matthew 10. 16–22; 10. 28–39; 16. 24–26;
    John 12. 24–26; 15. 18–21

Teachers of the Faith and Spiritual Writers
I Kings 3. [6–10] 11–14; Proverbs 4. 1–9;
    Wisdom 7. 7–10, 15–16; Ecclesiasticus 39. 1–10
Psalms 19. 7–10; 34. 11–17; 37. 31–35; 119. 89–96;
    119. 97–104
I Corinthians 1. 18–25; 2. 1–10; 2. 9–end;
    Ephesians 3. 8–12; 2 Timothy 4. 1–8; Titus 2. 1–8
Matthew 5. 13–19; 13. 52–end; 23. 8–12; Mark 4. 1–9;
    John 16. 12–15

Bishops and Other Pastors
I Samuel 16. I, 6–13; Isaiah 6. 1–8; Jeremiah 1. 4–10;
    Ezekiel 3. 16–21; Malachi 2. 5–7
Psalms 1; 15; 16. 5–end; 96; 110
Acts 20. 28–35; I Corinthians 4. 1–5;
    2 Corinthians 4. 1–10 (or 1–2, 5–7);
    5. 14–20; 1 Peter 5. 1–4

Matthew 11. 25–end; 24. 42–46; John 10. 11–16;
    15. 9–17; 21. 15–17

Members of Religious Communities
I Kings 19. 9–18; Proverbs 10. 27–end;
    Song of Solomon 8. 6–7; Isaiah 61.10 – 62.5;
    Hosea 2. 14–15, 19–20
Psalms 34. 1–8; 112. 1–9; 119. 57–64; 123; 131
Acts 4. 32–35; 2 Corinthians 10.17 – 11.2;
    Philippians 3. 7–14; 1 John 2. 15–17;
    Revelation 19. 1, 5–9
Matthew 11. 25–end; 19. 3–12; 19. 23–end;
    Luke 9. 57–end; 12. 32–37

Missionaries
Isaiah 52. 7–10; 61. 1–3a; Ezekiel 34. 11–16; Jonah 3. 1–5
Psalms 67; 87; 97; 100; 117
Acts 2. 14, 22–36; 13. 46–49; 16. 6–10; 26. 19–23;
    Romans 15. 17–21; 2 Corinthians 5.11 – 6.2
Matthew 9. 35–end; 28. 16–end; Mark 16. 15–20;
    Luke 5. 1–11; 10. 1–9

Any Saint
Genesis 12. 1–4; Proverbs 8. 1–11; Micah 6. 6–8;
    Ecclesiasticus 2. 7–13 [14–end]
Psalms 32; 33. 1–5; 119. 1–8; 139. 1–4 [5–12]; 145. 8–14
Ephesians 3. 14–19; 6. 11–18; Hebrews 13. 7–8, 15–16;
    James 2. 14–17; 1 John 4. 7–16; Revelation 21. [1–4]
    5–7
Matthew 19. 16–21; 25. 1–13; 25. 14–30; John 15. 1–8;
    17. 20–end

SPECIAL OCCASIONS

The Guidance of the Holy Spirit
Proverbs 24. 3–7; Isaiah 30. 15–21; Wisdom 9. 13–17
Psalms 25. 1–9; 104. 26–33; 143. 8–10
Acts 15. 23–29; Romans 8. 22–27;
   1 Corinthians 12. 4–13
Luke 14. 27–33; John 14. 23–26; 16. 13–15

The Commemoration of the Faithful Departed
Lamentations 3. 17–26, 31–33 or Wisdom 3. 1–9
Psalm 23 or 27. 1–6, 16–end
Romans 5. 5–11 or I Peter 1. 3–9
John 5. 19–25 or 6. 37–40

Rogation Days
Deuteronomy 8. 1–10; 1 Kings 8. 35–40; Job 28. 1–11
Psalms 104. 21–30; 107. 1–9; 121
Philippians 4. 4–7; 2 Thessalonians 3. 6–13;
   1 John 5. 12–15
Matthew 6. 1–15; Mark 11. 22–24; Luke 11. 5–13

Harvest Thanksgiving

Year A
Deuteronomy 8. 7–18 or 28. 1–14
Psalm 65
2 Corinthians 9. 6–end
Luke 12. 16–30 or 17. 11–19

Year B
Joel 2. 21–27
Psalm 126
1 Timothy 2. 1–7 or 6. 6–10
Matthew 6. 25–33

Year C
Deuteronomy 26. 1–11
Psalm 100
Philippians 4. 4–9 or Revelation 14. 14–18
John 6. 25–35

Mission and Evangelism
Isaiah 49. 1–6; 52. 7–10; Micah 4. 1–5
Psalms 2; 46; 67
Acts 17. 12–end; 2 Corinthians 5.14 – 6.2;
   Ephesians 2. 13–end
Matthew 5. 13–16; 28. 16–end; John 17. 20–end

The Unity of the Church
Jeremiah 33. 6–9a; Ezekiel 36. 23–28;
   Zephaniah 3. 16–end
Psalms 100; 122; 133
Ephesians 4. 1–6; Colossians 3. 9–17;
   1 John 4. 9–15
Matthew 18. 19–22; John 11. 45–52; 17. 11b–23

The Peace of the World
Isaiah 9. 1–6; 57. 15–19; Micah 4. 1–5
Psalms 40. 14–17; 72. 1–7; 85. 8–13
Philippians 4. 6–9; 1 Timothy 2. 1–6;
   James 3. 13–18
Matthew 5. 43–end; John 14. 23–29; 15. 9–17

Social Justice and Responsibility
Isaiah 32. 15–end; Amos 5. 21–24; 8. 4–7;
   Acts 5. 1–11
Psalms 31. 21–24; 85. 1–7; 146. 5–10
Colossians 3. 12–15; James 2. 1–4
Matthew 5. 1–12; 25. 31–end;
   Luke 16. 19–end

Ministry (including Ember Days)
Numbers 11. 16–17, 24–29; 27. 15–end;
   1 Samuel 16. 1–13a; Isaiah 6. 1–8; 61. 1–3;
   Jeremiah 1. 4–10
Psalms 40. 8–13; 84. 8–12; 89. 19–25;
   101. 1–5, 7; 122
Acts 20. 28–35; 1 Corinthians 3. 3–11;
   Ephesians 4. 4–16; Philippians 3. 7–14
Luke 4. 16–21; 12. 35–43; 22. 24–27;
   John 4. 31–38; 15. 5–17

In Time of Trouble
Genesis 9. 8–17; Job 1. 13–end; Isaiah 38. 6–11
Psalms 86. 1–7; 107. 4–15; 142. 1–7
Romans 3. 21–26; 8. 18–25;
   2 Corinthians 8. 1–5, 9
Mark 4. 35–end; Luke 12. 1–7; John 16. 31–end

For the Sovereign
Joshua 1. 1–9; Proverbs 8. 1–16
Psalms 20; 101; 121
Romans 13. 1–10; Revelation 21.22 – 22.4
Matthew 22. 16–22; Luke 22. 24–30

	Sunday Principal Service / Weekday Eucharist	Third Service / Morning Prayer	Second Service / Evening Prayer

27 Sunday   THE FIRST SUNDAY OF ADVENT
Common Worship Year A begins

P	Isa. 2. 1–5	Ps. 44	Ps. 9 (*or* 9. 1–8)
	Ps. 122	Mic. 4. 1–7	Isa. 52. 1–12
	Rom. 13. 11–end	1 Thess. 5. 1–11	Matt. 24. 15–28
	Matt. 24. 36–44		

28 Monday   Daily Eucharistic Lectionary Year 1 begins

P	Isa. 4. 2–end	Ps. *50*; 54	Ps. 70; *71*
	Ps. 122	*alt.* Ps. *1*; 2; 3	*alt.* Ps. *4*; 7
	Matt. 8. 5–11	Isa. 42. 18–end	Isa. 25. 1–9
		Rev. ch. 19	Matt. 12. 1–21

29 Tuesday

P	Isa. 11. 1–10	Ps. *80*; 82	Ps. *74*; 75
	Ps. 72. 1–4, 18–19	*alt.* Ps. *5*; 6; (8)	*alt.* Ps. *9*; 10†
	Luke 10. 21–24	Isa. 43. 1–13	Isa. 26. 1–13
		Rev. ch. 20	Matt. 12. 22–37
			or First EP of Andrew the Apostle
			Ps. 48
			Isa. 49. 1–9a
			1 Cor. 4. 9–16
			R ct

Day of Intercession and Thanksgiving for the Missionary Work of the Church:

Isa. 49. 1–6; Isa. 52. 7–10; Mic. 4. 1–5
Ps. 2; 46; 47
Acts 17. 12–end; 2 Cor. 5.14 – 6.2; Eph. 2. 13–end
Matt. 5. 13–16; Matt. 28. 16–end; John 17. 20–end

30 Wednesday   ANDREW THE APOSTLE

R	Isa. 52. 7–10	*MP*: Ps. 47; 147. 1–12	*EP*: Ps. 87; 96
	Ps. 19. 1–6	Ezek. 47. 1–12	Zech. 8. 20–end
	Rom. 10. 12–18	*or* Ecclus. 14. 20–end	John 1. 35–42
	Matt. 4. 18–22	John 12. 20–32	

December 2022

1 Thursday   *Charles de Foucauld, Hermit in the Sahara, 1916*

P	Isa. 26. 1–6	Ps. *42*; 43	Ps. *40*; 46
	Ps. 118. 18–27a	*alt.* Ps. 14; *15*; 16	*alt.* Ps. 18†
	Matt. 7. 21, 24–27	Isa. 44. 1–8	Isa. 28. 14–end
		Rev. 21. 9–21	Matt. 13. 1–23

2 Friday

P	Isa. 29. 17–end	Ps. *25*; 26	Ps. 16; *17*
	Ps. 27. 1–4, 16–17	*alt.* Ps. 17; *19*	*alt.* Ps. 22
	Matt. 9. 27–31	Isa. 44. 9–23	Isa. 29. 1–14
		Rev. 21.22 – 22.5	Matt. 13. 24–43

3 Saturday   *Francis Xavier, Missionary, Apostle of the Indies, 1552*

P	Isa. 30. 19–21, 23–26	Ps. *9*; (10)	Ps. *27*; 28
	Ps. 146. 4–9	*alt.* Ps. 20; 21; *23*	*alt.* Ps. *24*; 25
	Matt. 9.35 – 10.1, 6–8	Isa. 44.24 – 45.13	Isa. 29. 15–end
		Rev. 22. 6–end	Matt. 13. 44–end
			ct

Calendar and Holy Communion	Morning Prayer	Evening Prayer	**NOTES**
THE FIRST SUNDAY IN ADVENT Advent 1 Collect until Christmas Eve			
P Mic. 4. 1–4, 6–7 Ps. 25. 1–9 Rom. 13. 8–14 Matt. 21. 1–13	Ps. 44 Isa. 2. 1–5 1 Thess. 5. 1–11	Ps. 9 (or 9. 1–8) Isa. 52. 1–12 Matt. 24. 15–28	
P	Isa. 42. 18–end Rev. ch. 19	Isa. 25. 1–9 Matt. 12. 1–21	
P	Isa. 43. 1–13 Rev. ch. 20	Isa. 26. 1–13 Matt. 12. 22–37 *or First EP of Andrew the Apostle* (Ps. 48) Isa. 49. 1–9a 1 Cor. 4. 9–16	

R ct

To celebrate the Day of Intercession and Thanksgiving for the Missionary Work of the Church, see *Common Worship* provision.

ANDREW THE APOSTLE			
R Zech. 8. 20–end Ps. 92. 1–5 Rom. 10. 9–end Matt. 4. 18–22	(Ps. 47; 147. 1–12) Ezek. 47. 1–12 *or Ecclus.* 14. 20–end John 12. 20–32	(Ps. 87; 96) Isa. 52. 7–10 John 1. 35–42	
P	Isa. 44. 1–8 Rev. 21. 9–21	Isa. 28. 14–end Matt. 13. 1–23	
P	Isa. 44. 9–23 Rev. 21.22 – 22.5	Isa. 29. 1–14 Matt. 13. 24–43	
P	Isa. 44.24 – 45.13 Rev. 22. 6–end	Isa. 29. 15–end Matt. 13. 44–end	

ct

		Sunday Principal Service Weekday Eucharist	Third Service Morning Prayer	Second Service Evening Prayer
4 Sunday	THE SECOND SUNDAY OF ADVENT			
P		Isa. 11. 1–10 Ps. 72. 1–7, 18–19 (*or* 72. 1–7) Rom. 15. 4–13 Matt. 3. 1–12	Ps. 80 Amos ch. 7 Luke 1. 5–20	Ps. 11; [28] 1 Kings 18. 17–39 John 1. 19–28
5 Monday				
P		Isa. ch. 35 Ps. 85. 7–end Luke 5. 17–26	Ps. 44 *alt.* Ps. 27; *30* Isa. 45. 14–end 1 Thess. ch. 1	Ps. *144*; 146 *alt.* Ps. 26; *28*; 29 Isa. 30. 1–18 Matt. 14. 1–12
6 Tuesday	Nicholas, Bishop of Myra, *c.* 326			
Pw		Com. Bishop *or* *also* Isa. 61. 1–3 1 Tim. 6. 6–11 Mark 10. 13–16	Isa. 40. 1–11 Ps. 96. 1, 10–end Matt. 18. 12–14	Ps. *56*; 57 *alt.* Ps. 32; *36* Isa. ch. 46 1 Thess. 2. 1–12	Ps. *11*; 12; 13 *alt.* Ps. 33 Isa. 30. 19–end Matt. 14. 13–end
7 Wednesday	Ambrose, Bishop of Milan, Teacher, 397. Ember Day*			
Pw		Com. Teacher *or* *also* Isa. 41. 9b–13 Luke 22. 24–30	Isa. 40. 25–end Ps. 103. 8–13 Matt. 11. 28–end	Ps. *62*; 63 *alt.* Ps. 34 Isa. ch. 47 1 Thess. 2. 13–end	Ps. *10*; 14 *alt.* Ps. 119. 33–56 Isa. ch. 31 Matt. 15. 1–20
8 Thursday	The Conception of the Blessed Virgin Mary			
Pw		Com. BVM *or* Ps. 145. 1, 8–13 Matt. 11. 11–15	Isa. 41. 13–20	Ps. 53; *54*; 60 *alt.* Ps. 37† Isa. 48. 1–11 1 Thess. ch. 3	Ps. 73 *alt.* Ps. 39; *40* Isa. ch. 32 Matt. 15. 21–28
9 Friday	Ember Day*			
P		Isa. 48. 17–19 Ps. 1 Matt. 11. 16–19	Ps. 85; *86* *alt.* Ps. 31 Isa. 48. 12–end 1 Thess. 4. 1–12	Ps. 82; *90* *alt.* Ps. 35 Isa. 33. 1–22 Matt. 15. 29–end
10 Saturday	Ember Day*			
P		Ecclus. 48. 1–4, 9–11 *or* 2 Kings 2. 9–12 Ps. 80. 1–4, 18–19 Matt. 17. 10–13	Ps. 145 *alt.* Ps. 41; *42*; 43 Isa. 49. 1–13 1 Thess. 4. 13–end	Ps. 93; *94* *alt.* Ps. 45; *46* Isa. ch. 35 Matt. 16. 1–12 ct
11 Sunday	THE THIRD SUNDAY OF ADVENT			
P		Isa. 35. 1–10 Ps. 146. 4–10 *or Canticle*: Magnificat Jas. 5. 7–10 Matt. 11. 2–11	Ps. 68. 1–19 Zeph. 3. 14–end Phil. 4. 4–7	Ps. 12; [14] Isa. 5. 8–end Acts 13. 13–41 *Gospel*: John 5. 31–40
12 Monday				
P		Num. 24. 2–7, 15–17 Ps. 25. 3–8 Matt. 21. 23–27	Ps. 40 *alt.* Ps. 44 Isa. 49. 14–25 1 Thess. 5. 1–11	Ps. 25; *26* *alt.* Ps. *47*; 49 Isa. 38. 1–8, 21–22 Matt. 16. 13–end

* For Ember Day provision, see p. 11.

Calendar and Holy Communion	Morning Prayer	Evening Prayer	NOTES
THE SECOND SUNDAY IN ADVENT			
P 2 Kings 22. 8–10; 23. 1–3 Ps. 50. 1–6 Rom. 15. 4–13 Luke 21. 25–33	Ps. 80 Amos ch. 7 Luke 1. 5–20	Ps. 11; [28] 1 Kings 18. 17–39 Matt. 3. 1–12	
P	Isa. 45. 14–end 1 Thess. ch. 1	Isa. 30. 1–18 Matt. 14. 1–12	
Nicholas, Bishop of Myra, c. 326			
Pw Com. Bishop	Isa. ch. 46 1 Thess. 2. 1–12	Isa. 30. 19–end Matt. 14. 13–end	
P	Isa. ch. 47 1 Thess. 2. 13–end	Isa. ch. 31 Matt. 15. 1–20	
The Conception of the Blessed Virgin Mary			
Pw	Isa. 48. 1–11 1 Thess. ch. 3	Isa. ch. 32 Matt. 15. 21–28	
P	Isa. 48. 12–end 1 Thess. 4. 1–12	Isa. 33. 1–22 Matt. 15. 29–end	
P	Isa. 49. 1–13 1 Thess. 4. 13–end	Isa. ch. 35 Matt. 16. 1–12	
		ct	
THE THIRD SUNDAY IN ADVENT			
P Isa. ch. 35 Ps. 80. 1–7 1 Cor. 4. 1–5 Matt. 11. 2–10	Ps. 68. 1–19 Zeph. 3. 14–end Jas. 5. 7–10	Ps. 12; [14] Isa. 5. 8–end Acts 13. 13–41	
P	Isa. 49. 14–25 1 Thess. 5. 1–11	Isa. 38. 1–8, 21–22 Matt. 16. 13–end	

		Sunday Principal Service Weekday Eucharist	Third Service Morning Prayer	Second Service Evening Prayer

13 Tuesday   Lucy, Martyr at Syracuse, 304
Samuel Johnson, Moralist, 1784

Pr	Com. Martyr *or* *also* Wisd. 3. 1–7 2 Cor. 4. 6–15	Zeph. 3. 1–2, 9–13 Ps. 34. 1–6, 21–22 Matt. 21. 28–32	Ps. **70**; 74 *alt*. Ps. **48**; 52 Isa. ch. 50 1 Thess. 5. 12–end	Ps. **50**; 54 *alt*. Ps. 50 Isa. 38. 9–20 Matt. 17. 1–13

14 Wednesday   John of the Cross, Poet, Teacher, 1591

Pw	Com. Teacher *or* *esp.* 1 Cor. 2. 1–10 *also* John 14. 18–23	Isa. 45. 6b–8, 18, 21b–end Ps. 85. 7–end Luke 7. 18b–23	Ps. **75**; 96 *alt*. Ps. 119. 57–80 Isa. 51. 1–8 2 Thess. ch. 1	Ps. 25; **82** *alt*. Ps. **59**; 60; (67) Isa. ch. 39 Matt. 17. 14–21

15 Thursday

P		Isa. 54. 1–10 Ps. 30. 1–5, 11–end Luke 7. 24–30	Ps. **76**; 97 *alt*. Ps. 56; **57**; (63†) Isa. 51. 9–16 2 Thess. ch. 2	Ps. 44 *alt*. Ps. 61; **62**; 64 Zeph. 1.1 – 2.3 Matt. 17. 22–end

16 Friday

P		Isa. 56. 1–3a, 6–8 Ps. 67 John 5. 33–36	Ps. 77; **98** *alt*. Ps. **51**; 54 Isa. 51. 17–end 2 Thess. ch. 3	Ps. 49 *alt*. Ps. 38 Zeph. 3. 1–13 Matt. 18. 1–20

17 Saturday   O Sapientia
Eglantyne Jebb, Social Reformer, Founder of 'Save the Children', 1928

P		Gen. 49. 2, 8–10 Ps. 72. 1–5, 18–19 Matt. 1. 1–17	Ps. 71 *alt*. Ps. 68 Isa. 52. 1–12 Jude	Ps. 42; **43** *alt*. Ps. 65; **66** Zeph. 3. 14–end Matt. 18. 21–end ct

18 Sunday   THE FOURTH SUNDAY OF ADVENT

P		Isa. 7. 10–16 Ps. 80. 1–8, 18–20 (*or* 80. 1–8) Rom. 1. 1–7 Matt. 1. 18–end	Ps. 144 Mic. 5. 2–5a Luke 1. 26–38	Ps. 113; [126] 1 Sam. 1. 1–20 Rev. 22. 6–end *Gospel*: Luke 1. 39–45

19 Monday

P		Judg. 13. 2–7, 24–end Ps. 71. 3–8 Luke 1. 5–25	Ps. 144; **146** Isa. 52.13 – 53.end 2 Pet. 1. 1–15	Ps. 10; **57** Mal. 1. 1, 6–end Matt. 19. 1–12

20 Tuesday

P		Isa. 7. 10–14 Ps. 24. 1–6 Luke 1. 26–38	Ps. **46**; 95 Isa. ch. 54 2 Pet. 1.16 – 2.3	Ps. **4**; 9 Mal. 2. 1–16 Matt. 19. 13–15

21 Wednesday*

P		Zeph. 3. 14–18 Ps. 33. 1–4, 11–12, 20–end Luke 1. 39–45	Ps. **121**; 122; 123 Isa. ch. 55 2 Pet. 2. 4–end	Ps. 80; **84** Mal. 2.17 – 3.12 Matt. 19. 16–end

*Thomas the Apostle may be celebrated on 21 December instead of 3 July.

	Calendar and Holy Communion	Morning Prayer	Evening Prayer	**NOTES**
	Lucy, Martyr at Syracuse, 304			
Pr	Com. Virgin Martyr	Isa. ch. 50 1 Thess. 5. 12–end	Isa. 38. 9–20 Matt. 17. 1–13	
	Ember Day			
P	Ember CEG	Isa. 51. 1–8 2 Thess. ch. 1	Isa. ch. 39 Matt. 17. 14–21	
P		Isa. 51. 9–16 2 Thess. ch. 2	Zeph. 1.1 – 2.3 Matt. 17. 22–end	
	O Sapientia Ember Day			
P	Ember CEG	Isa. 51. 17–end 2 Thess. ch. 3	Zeph. 3. 1–13 Matt. 18. 1–20	
	Ember Day			
P	Ember CEG	Isa. 52. 1–12 Jude	Zeph. 3. 14–end Matt. 18. 21–end	
			ct	
	THE FOURTH SUNDAY IN ADVENT			
P	Isa. 40. 1–9 Ps. 145. 17–end Phil. 4. 4–7 John 1. 19–28	Ps. 144 Mic. 5. 2–5a Luke 1. 26–38	Ps. 113; [126] 1 Sam. 1. 1–20 Rev. 22. 6–end	
P		Isa. 52.13 – 53.end 2 Pet. 1. 1–15	Mal. 1. 1, 6–end Matt. 19. 1–12	
P		Isa. ch. 54 2 Pet. 1.16 – 2.3	Mal. 2. 1–16 Matt. 19. 13–15 *or First EP of Thomas* (Ps. 27) Isa. ch. 35 Heb. 10.35 – 11.1 **R ct**	
	THOMAS THE APOSTLE			
R	Job 42. 1–6 Ps. 139. 1–11 Eph. 2. 19–end John 20. 24–end	(Ps. 92; 146) 2 Sam. 15. 17–21 *or* Ecclus. ch. 2 John 11. 1–16	(Ps. 139) Hab. 2. 1–4 1 Pet. 1. 3–12	

	Sunday Principal Service Weekday Eucharist	Third Service Morning Prayer	Second Service Evening Prayer
22 Thursday			
P	1 Sam. 1. 24–end Ps. 113 Luke 1. 46–56	Ps. *124*; 125; 126; 127 Isa. 56. 1–8 2 Pet. ch. 3	Ps. 24; *48* Mal. 3.13 – 4.end Matt. 23. 1–12
23 Friday			
P	Mal. 3. 1–4; 4. 5–end Ps. 25. 3–9 Luke 1. 57–66	Ps. 128; 129; *130*; 131 Isa. 63. 1–6 2 John	Ps. 89. 1–37 Nahum ch. 1 Matt. 23. 13–28
24 Saturday **CHRISTMAS EVE**			
P	*Morning Eucharist* 2 Sam. 7. 1–5, 8–11, 16 Ps. 89. 2, 19–27 Acts 13. 16–26 Luke 1. 67–79	Ps. *45*; 113 Isa. ch. 58 3 John	Ps. 85 Zech. ch. 2 Rev. 1. 1–8
25 Sunday **CHRISTMAS DAY**			
𝖜	*Any of the following sets of readings may be used on the evening of Christmas Eve and on Christmas Day. Set III should be used at some service during the celebration.* *I* Isa. 9. 2–7 Ps. 96 Titus 2. 11–14 Luke 2. 1–14 [15–20] *II* Isa. 62. 6–end Ps. 97 Titus 3. 4–7 Luke 2. [1–7] 8–20 *III* Isa. 52. 7–10 Ps. 98 Heb. 1. 1–4 [5–12] John 1. 1–14	*MP*: Ps. *110*; 117 Isa. 62. 1–5 Matt. 1. 18–end	*EP*: Ps. 8 Isa. 65. 17–25 Phil. 2. 5–11 or Luke 2. 1–20 *if it has not been used at the principal service of the day*
26 Monday **STEPHEN, DEACON, FIRST MARTYR**			
R	2 Chron. 24. 20–22 or Acts 7. 51–end Ps. 119. 161–168 Acts 7. 51–end or Gal. 2. 16b–20 Matt. 10. 17–22	*MP*: Ps. *13*; 31. 1–8; 150 Jer. 26. 12–15 Acts ch. 6	*EP*: Ps. 57; *86* Gen. 4. 1–10 Matt. 23. 34–end
27 Tuesday **JOHN, APOSTLE AND EVANGELIST**			
W	Exod. 33. 7–11a Ps. 117 1 John ch. 1 John 21. 19b–end	*MP*: Ps. *21*; 147. 13–end Exod. 33. 12–end 1 John 2. 1–11	*EP*: Ps. 97 Isa. 6. 1–8 1 John 5. 1–12

	Calendar and Holy Communion	Morning Prayer	Evening Prayer	NOTES
P		Isa. 56. 1–8 2 Pet. ch. 3	Mal. 3.13 – 4.end Matt. 23. 1–12	
P		Isa. 63. 1–6 2 John	Nahum ch. 1 Matt. 23. 13–28	

CHRISTMAS EVE

	Calendar and Holy Communion	Morning Prayer	Evening Prayer	NOTES
P	Collect (1) Christmas Eve (2) Advent 1 Mic. 5. 2–5a Ps. 24 Titus 3. 3–7 Luke 2. 1–14	Isa. ch. 58 3 John	Zech. ch. 2 Rev. 1. 1–8	

CHRISTMAS DAY

	Calendar and Holy Communion	Morning Prayer	Evening Prayer	NOTES
W	Isa. 9. 2–7 Ps. 98 Heb. 1. 1–12 John 1. 1–14	Ps. 110; 117 Isa. 62. 1–5 Matt. 1. 18–end	Ps. 8 Isa. 65. 17–25 Phil. 2. 5–11 or Luke 2. 1–20	

STEPHEN, DEACON, FIRST MARTYR

	Calendar and Holy Communion	Morning Prayer	Evening Prayer	NOTES
R	Collect (1) Stephen (2) Christmas 2 Chron. 24. 20–22 Ps. 119. 161–168 Acts 7. 55–end Matt. 23. 34–end	(Ps. 13; 31. 1–8; 150) Jer. 26. 12–15 Acts ch. 6	(Ps. 57; 86) Gen. 4. 1–10 Matt. 10. 17–22	

JOHN, APOSTLE AND EVANGELIST

	Calendar and Holy Communion	Morning Prayer	Evening Prayer	NOTES
W	Collect (1) John (2) Christmas Exod. 33. 18–end Ps. 92. 11–end 1 John ch. 1 John 21. 19b–end	(Ps. 21; 147. 13–end) Exod. 33. 7–11a 1 John 2. 1–11	(Ps. 97) Isa. 6. 1–8 1 John 5. 1–12	

	Sunday Principal Service Weekday Eucharist	Third Service Morning Prayer	Second Service Evening Prayer

28 Wednesday   **THE HOLY INNOCENTS**

R	Jer. 31. 15–17 Ps. 124 1 Cor. 1. 26–29 Matt. 2. 13–18	MP: Ps. **36**; 146 Baruch 4. 21–27 or Gen. 37. 13–20 Matt. 18. 1–10	EP: Ps. 123; **128** Isa. 49. 14–25 Mark 10. 13–16

29 Thursday   **Thomas Becket, Archbishop of Canterbury, Martyr, 1170***

Wr	Com. Martyr or *esp.* Matt. 10. 28–33 *also* Ecclus. 51. 1–8	1 John 2. 3–11 Ps. 96. 1–4 Luke 2. 22–35	Ps. **19**; 20 Isa. 57. 15–end John 1. 1–18	Ps. 131; **132** Jonah ch. 1 Col. 1. 1–14

30 Friday

W		1 John 2. 12–17 Ps. 96. 7–10 Luke 2. 36–40	Ps. 111; 112; **113** Isa. 59. 1–15a John 1. 19–28	Ps. **65**; 84 Jonah ch. 2 Col. 1. 15–23

31 Saturday   *John Wyclif, Reformer, 1384*

W		1 John 2. 18–21 Ps. 96. 1, 11–end John 1. 1–18	Ps. 102 Isa. 59. 15b–end John 1. 29–34	Ps. **90**; 148 Jonah chs 3 & 4 Col. 1.24 – 2.7 *or First EP of The* *Naming of Jesus* Ps. 148 Jer. 23. 1–6 Col. 2. 8–15 **ct**

January 2023

1 Sunday   **THE NAMING AND CIRCUMCISION OF JESUS** (or transferred to 2 January)
or **THE SECOND SUNDAY OF CHRISTMAS**

W	Num. 6. 22–end Ps. 8 Gal. 4. 4–7 Luke 2. 15–21	MP: Ps. **103**; 150 Gen. 17. 1–13 Rom. 2. 17–end	EP: Ps. 115 Deut. 30. [1–10] 11–end Acts 3. 1–16

W	*or, for The Second Sunday of Christmas:* Isa. 63. 7–9 Ps. 148 (or 148. 7–end) Heb. 2. 10–end Matt. 2. 13–end	Ps. 105. 1–11 Isa. 35. 1–6 Gal. 2. 23–end	Ps. 132 Isa. 49. 7–13 Phil. 2. 1–11 *Gospel:* Luke 2. 41–52

2 Monday   **Basil the Great and Gregory of Nazianzus, Bishops, Teachers, 379 and 389**
Seraphim, Monk of Sarov, Spiritual Guide, 1833; Vedanayagam Samuel Azariah, Bishop in South India,
Evangelist, 1945
For The Naming and Circumcision of Jesus, see provision for 31 December and 1 January.

W	Com. Teacher or *esp.* 2 Tim. 4. 1–8 Matt. 5. 13–19	1 John 2. 22–28 Ps. 98. 1–4 John 1. 19–28	Ps. 18. 1–30 Isa. 60. 1–12 John 1. 35–42	Ps. 45; **46** Ruth ch. 1 Col. 2. 8–end

3 Tuesday

W		1 John 2.29 – 3.6 Ps. 98. 2–7 John 1. 29–34	Ps. **127**; 128; 131 Isa. 60. 13–end John 1. 43–end	Ps. **2**; 110 Ruth ch. 2 Col. 3. 1–11

*Thomas Becket may be celebrated on 7 July instead of 29 December.

	Calendar and Holy Communion	Morning Prayer	Evening Prayer	NOTES
	THE HOLY INNOCENTS			
R	Collect (1) Innocents (2) Christmas Jer. 31. 10–17 Ps. 123 Rev. 14. 1–5 Matt. 2. 13–18	(Ps. 36; 146) Baruch 4. 21–27 or Gen. 37. 13–20 Matt. 18. 1–10	(Ps. 124; 128) Isa. 49. 14–25 Mark 10. 13–16	
W	CEG of Christmas	Isa. 57. 15–end John 1. 1–18	Jonah ch. 1 Col. 1. 1–14	
W	CEG of Christmas	Isa. 59. 1–15a John 1. 19–28	Jonah ch. 2 Col. 1. 15–23	
	Silvester, Bishop of Rome, 335			
W	Com. Bishop	Isa. 59. 15b–end John 1. 29–34	Jonah chs 3 & 4 Col. 1.24 – 2.7 or First EP of The Circumcision of Christ Ps. 148 Jer. 23. 1–6 Col. 2. 8–15	
			ct	
	THE CIRCUMCISION OF CHRIST (or transferred to 2 January)			
W	Additional collect Gen. 17. 3b–10 Ps. 98 Rom. 4. 8–13 or Eph. 2. 11–18 Luke 2. 15–21	Ps. 103; 150 Gen. 17. 1–13 Rom. 2. 17–end	Ps. 115 Deut. 30. [1–10] 11–end Acts 3. 1–16	
	or, for The Sunday after Christmas Day:			
W	Isa. 62. 10–12 Ps. 45. 1–7 Gal. 4. 1–7 Matt. 1. 18–end	Ps. 105. 1–11 Isa. 35. 1–6 Gal. 2. 23–end	Ps. 132 Isa. 49. 7–13 Phil. 2. 1–11	
W		Isa. 60. 1–12 John 1. 35–42	Ruth ch. 1 Col. 2. 8–end	
W		Isa. 60. 13–end John 1. 43–end	Ruth ch. 2 Col. 3. 1–11	

		Sunday Principal Service Weekday Eucharist	Third Service Morning Prayer	Second Service Evening Prayer
4 Wednesday				
W		1 John 3. 7–10 Ps. 98. 1, 8–end John 1. 35–42	Ps. 89. 1–37 Isa. ch. 61 John 2. 1–12	Ps. 85; *87* Ruth ch. 3 Col. 3.12 – 4. 1
5 Thursday				
W		1 John 3. 11–21 Ps. 100 John 1. 43–end	Ps. 8; *48* Isa. ch. 62 John 2. 13–end	*First EP of The* *Epiphany* Ps. 96; *97* Isa. 49. 1–13 John 4. 7–26 𝖂 ct *or, if The Epiphany* *is celebrated on 8* *January*: Ps. 96; *97* Ruth 4. 1–17 Col. 4. 2–end
6 Friday **THE EPIPHANY**				
𝖂		Isa. 60. 1–6 Ps. 72. 1–15 (or 72. 10–15) Eph. 3. 1–12 Matt. 2. 1–12	*MP*: Ps. ***132***; 113 Jer. 31. 7–14 John 1. 29–34	*EP*: Ps. *98*; 100 Baruch 4.36 – 5.end or Isa. 60. 1–9 John 2. 1–11
	or, if The Epiphany is celebrated on 8 January:			
W		1 John 5. 5–13 Ps. 147. 13–end Mark 1. 7–11	Ps. 46; 147. 13–end Isa. 63. 7–end 1 John ch. 3	Ps. 145 Baruch 1.15 – 2.10 or Jer. 23. 1–8 Matt. 20. 1–16
7 Saturday				
W		1 John 3.22 – 4.6 Ps. 2. 7–end Matt. 4. 12–17, 23–end	Ps. *99*; 147. 1–12 *alt.* Ps. *76*; 79 Isa. 63. 7–end 1 John ch. 3	*First EP of The Baptism* *of Christ* Ps. 36 Isa. ch. 61 Titus 2. 11–14; 3. 4–7 𝖂 ct
	or, if The Epiphany is celebrated on 8 January:			
W		1 John 5. 14–end Ps. 149. 1–5 John 2. 1–11	Ps. *99*; 147. 1–12 Isa. ch. 64 1 John 4. 7–end	*First EP of The* *Epiphany* Ps. 96; *97* Isa. 49. 1–13 John 4. 7–26 𝖂 ct
8 Sunday **THE BAPTISM OF CHRIST (THE FIRST SUNDAY OF EPIPHANY)**				
or transferred to 9 January if The Epiphany is celebrated today. (For The Epiphany, see provision on 6 January.)				
𝖂		Isa. 42. 1–9 Ps. 29 Acts 10. 34–43 Matt. 3. 13–end	Ps. 89. 19–29 Exod. 14. 15–22 1 John 5. 6–9	Ps. 46; 47 Josh. 3. 1–8, 14–end Heb. 1. 1–12 *Gospel*: Luke 3. 15–22
9 Monday	For the Baptism of Christ, see provision for the 7 and 8 January.			
W DEL 1		Heb. 1. 1–6 Ps. 97. 1–2, 6–10 Mark 1. 14–20	Ps. *2*; 110 *alt.* Ps. *80*; 82 Amos ch. 1 1 Cor. 1. 1–17	Ps. *34*; 36 *alt.* Ps. *85*; 86 Gen. 1. 1–19 Matt. 21. 1–17

	Calendar and Holy Communion	Morning Prayer	Evening Prayer	NOTES
W		Isa. ch. 61 John 2. 1–12	Ruth ch. 3 Col. 3.12 – 4. 1	
W		Isa. ch. 62 John 2. 13–end	*First EP of The Epiphany* Ps. 96; 97 Isa. 49. 1–13 John 4. 7–26 𝔚 ct	

THE EPIPHANY

	Calendar and Holy Communion	Morning Prayer	Evening Prayer	NOTES
𝔚	Isa. 60. 1–9 Ps. 100 Eph. 3. 1–12 Matt. 2. 1–12	Ps. 132; 113 Jer. 31. 7–14 John 1. 29–34	Ps. 72; 98 Baruch 4.36 – 5.end or Isa. 60. 1–9 John 2. 1–11	
W *or* **G**		Isa. 63. 7–end 1 John ch. 3	Baruch 1.15 – 2.10 or Jer. 23. 1–8 Matt. 20. 1–16 ct	

THE FIRST SUNDAY AFTER THE EPIPHANY
To celebrate The Baptism of Christ, see *Common Worship* provision.

	Calendar and Holy Communion	Morning Prayer	Evening Prayer	NOTES
W *or* **G**	Zech. 8. 1–8 Ps. 72. 1–8 Rom. 12. 1–5 Luke 2. 41–end	Ps. 89. 19–29 Exod. 14. 15–22 1 John 5. 6–9	Ps. 46; 47 Josh. 3. 1–8, 14–end Heb. 1. 1–12	
W *or* **G**		Amos ch. 1 1 Cor. 1. 1–17	Gen. 1. 1–19 Matt. 21. 1–17	

		Sunday Principal Service Weekday Eucharist	Third Service Morning Prayer	Second Service Evening Prayer

10 Tuesday *William Laud, Archbishop of Canterbury, 1645*

W		Heb. 2. 5–12 Ps. 8 Mark 1. 21–28	Ps. 8; *9* *alt.* Ps. 87; **89. 1–18** Amos ch. 2 1 Cor. 1. 18–end	Ps. **45**; 46 *alt.* Ps. 89. 19–end Gen. 1.20 – 2.3 Matt. 21. 18–32

11 Wednesday *Mary Slessor, Missionary in West Africa, 1915*

W		Heb. 2. 14–end Ps. 105. 1–9 Mark 1. 29–39	Ps. 19; *20* *alt.* Ps. 119. 105–128 Amos ch. 3 1 Cor. ch. 2	Ps. **47**; 48 *alt.* Ps. **91**; 93 Gen. 2. 4–end Matt. 21. 33–end

12 Thursday **Aelred of Hexham, Abbot of Rievaulx, 1167**
Benedict Biscop, Abbot of Wearmouth, Scholar, 689

W	Com. Religious *or* *also* Ecclus. 15. 1–6	Heb. 3. 7–14 Ps. 95. 1, 8–end Mark 1. 40–end	Ps. *21*; 24 *alt.* Ps. 90; *92* Amos ch. 4 1 Cor. ch. 3	Ps. *61*; 65 *alt.* Ps. 94 Gen. ch. 3 Matt. 22. 1–14

13 Friday **Hilary, Bishop of Poitiers, Teacher, 367**
Kentigern (Mungo), Missionary Bishop in Strathclyde and Cumbria, 603; George Fox, Founder of the Society of Friends (the Quakers), 1691

W	Com. Teacher *or* *also* 1 John 2. 18–25 John 8. 25–32	Heb. 4. 1–5, 11 Ps. 78. 3–8 Mark 2. 1–12	Ps. *67*; 72 *alt.* Ps. *88*; (95) Amos 5. 1–17 1 Cor. ch. 4	Ps. 68 *alt.* Ps. 102 Gen. 4. 1–16, 25–26 Matt. 22. 15–33

14 Saturday

W		Heb. 4. 12–end Ps. 19. 7–end Mark 2. 13–17	Ps. 29; *33* *alt.* Ps. 96; *97*; 100 Amos 5. 18–end 1 Cor. ch. 5	Ps. 84; *85* *alt.* Ps. 104 Gen. 6. 1–10 Matt. 22. 34–end ct

15 Sunday **THE SECOND SUNDAY OF EPIPHANY**

W		Isa. 49. 1–7 Ps. 40. 1–12 1 Cor. 1. 1–9 John 1. 29–42	Ps. 145. 1–12 Jer. 1. 4–10 Mark 1. 14–20	Ps. 96 Ezek. 2.1 – 3.4 Gal. 1. 11–end *Gospel:* John 1. 43–end

16 Monday

W **DEL 2**		Heb. 5. 1–10 Ps. 110. 1–4 Mark 2. 18–22	Ps. 145; *146* *alt.* Ps. *98*; 99; 101 Amos ch. 6 1 Cor. 6. 1–11	Ps. 71 *alt.* Ps. 105† (*or* Ps. 103) Gen. 6.11 – 7.10 Matt. 24. 1–14

17 Tuesday **Antony of Egypt, Hermit, Abbot, 356**
Charles Gore, Bishop, Founder of the Community of the Resurrection, 1932

W	Com. Religious *or* *esp.* Phil. 3. 7–14 *also* Matt. 19. 16–26	Heb. 6. 10–end Ps. 111 Mark 2. 23–end	Ps. *132*; 147. 1–12 *alt.* Ps. 106† (*or* Ps. 103) Amos ch. 7 1 Cor. 6. 12–end	Ps. 89. 1–37 *alt.* Ps. 107† Gen. 7. 11–end Matt. 24. 15–28

18 Wednesday *Amy Carmichael, Founder of the Dohnavur Fellowship, Spiritual Writer, 1951*
The Week of Prayer for Christian Unity until 25 January

W		Heb. 7. 1–3, 15–17 Ps. 110. 1–4 Mark 3. 1–6	Ps. *81*; 147. 13–end *alt.* Ps. 110; *111*; 112 Amos ch. 8 1 Cor. 7. 1–24	Ps. *97*; 98 *alt.* Ps. 119. 129–152 Gen. 8. 1–14 Matt. 24. 29–end

	Calendar and Holy Communion	Morning Prayer	Evening Prayer	NOTES
W or **G**		Amos ch. 2 1 Cor. 1. 18–end	Gen. 1.20 – 2.3 Matt. 21. 18–32	
W or **G**		Amos ch. 3 1 Cor. ch. 2	Gen. 2. 4–end Matt. 21. 33–end	
W or **G**		Amos ch. 4 1 Cor. ch. 3	Gen. ch. 3 Matt. 22. 1–14	

Hilary, Bishop of Poitiers, Teacher, 367

	Calendar and Holy Communion	Morning Prayer	Evening Prayer	
W or **Gw**	Com. Doctor	Amos 5. 1–17 1 Cor. ch. 4	Gen. 4. 1–16, 25–26 Matt. 22. 15–33	
W or **G**		Amos 5. 18–end 1 Cor. ch. 5	Gen. 6. 1–10 Matt. 22. 34–end	
			ct	

THE SECOND SUNDAY AFTER THE EPIPHANY

	Calendar and Holy Communion	Morning Prayer	Evening Prayer	
W or **G**	2 Kings 4. 1–17 Ps. 107. 13–22 Rom. 12. 6–16a John 2. 1–11	Ps. 145. 1–12 Jer. 1. 4–10 Mark 1. 14–20	Ps. 96 Ezek. 2.1 – 3.4 Gal. 1. 11–end	
W or **G**		Amos ch. 6 1 Cor. 6. 1–11	Gen. 6.11 – 7.10 Matt. 24. 1–14	
W or **G**		Amos ch. 7 1 Cor. 6. 12–end	Gen. 7. 11–end Matt. 24. 15–28	

Prisca, Martyr at Rome, c. 265
For the Week of Prayer for Christian Unity, see *Common Worship* provision.

	Calendar and Holy Communion	Morning Prayer	Evening Prayer	
Wr or **Gr**	Com. Virgin Martyr	Amos ch. 8 1 Cor. 7. 1–24	Gen. 8. 1–14 Matt. 24. 29–end	

		Sunday Principal Service Weekday Eucharist	Third Service Morning Prayer	Second Service Evening Prayer
19 Thursday	**Wulfstan, Bishop of Worcester, 1095**			
W	Com. Bishop *or* *esp.* Matt. 24. 42–46	Heb. 7.25 – 8.6 Ps. 40. 7–10, 17–end Mark 3. 7–12	Ps. *76*; 148 *alt.* Ps. 113; *115* Amos ch. 9 1 Cor. 7. 25–end	Ps. 99; 100; *111* *alt.* Ps. 114; *116*; 117 Gen. 8.15 – 9.7 Matt. 25. 1–13
20 Friday	*Richard Rolle of Hampole, Spiritual Writer, 1349*			
W		Heb. 8. 6–end Ps. 85. 7–end Mark 3. 13–19	Ps. *27*; 149 *alt.* Ps. 139 Hos. 1.1 – 2.1 1 Cor. ch. 8	Ps. 73 *alt.* Ps. *130*; 131; 137 Gen. 9. 8–19 Matt. 25. 14–30
21 Saturday	**Agnes, Child Martyr at Rome, 304**			
Wr	Com. Martyr *or* *also* Rev. 7. 13–end	Heb. 9. 2–3, 11–14 Ps. 47. 1–8 Mark 3. 20–21	Ps. *122*; 128; 150 *alt.* Ps. 120; *121*; 122 Hos. 2. 2–17 1 Cor. 9. 1–14	Ps. *61*; 66 *alt.* Ps. 118 Gen. 11. 1–9 Matt. 25. 31–end **ct**
22 Sunday	**THE THIRD SUNDAY OF EPIPHANY**			
W		Isa. 9. 1–4 Ps. 27. 1, 4–12 (*or* 27. 1–11) 1 Cor. 1. 10–18 Matt. 4. 12–23	Ps. 113 Amos 3. 1–8 1 John 1. 1–4	Ps. 33 (*or* 33. 1–12) Eccles. 3. 1–11 1 Pet. 1. 3–12 *Gospel:* Luke 4. 14–21
23 Monday **DEL 3**		Heb. 9. 15, 24–end Ps. 98. 1–7 Mark 3. 22–30	Ps. 40; *108* *alt.* Ps. 123; 124; 125; *126* Hos. 2.18 – 3.end 1 Cor. 9. 15–end	Ps. *138*; 144 *alt.* Ps. *127*; 128; 129 Gen. 11.27 – 12.9 Matt. 26. 1–16
W				
24 Tuesday	**Francis de Sales, Bishop of Geneva, Teacher, 1622**			
W	Com. Teacher *or* *also* Prov. 3. 13–18 John 3. 17–21	Heb. 10. 1–10 Ps. 40. 1–4, 7–10 Mark 3. 31–end	Ps. 34; *36* *alt.* Ps. *132*; 133 Hos. 4. 1–16 1 Cor. 10. 1–13	Ps. 145 *alt.* Ps. (134); *135* Gen. 13. 2–end Matt. 26. 17–35 *or First EP of The Conversion of Paul* Ps. 149 Isa. 49. 1–13 Acts 22. 3–16 **ct**
25 Wednesday	**THE CONVERSION OF PAUL**			
W		Jer. 1. 4–10 *or* Acts 9. 1–22 Ps. 67 Acts 9. 1–22 *or* Gal. 1. 11–16a Matt. 19. 27–end	*MP:* Ps. 66; 147. 13–end Ezek. 3. 22–end Phil. 3. 1–14	*EP:* Ps. 119. 41–56 Ecclus. 39. 1–10 *or* Isa. 56. 1–8 Col. 1.24 – 2.7
26 Thursday	**Timothy and Titus, Companions of Paul**			
W	Isa. 61. 1–3a *or* Ps. 100 2 Tim. 2. 1–8 *or* Titus 1. 1–5 Luke 10. 1–9	Heb. 10. 19–25 Ps. 24. 1–6 Mark 4. 21–25	Ps. *47*; 48 *alt.* Ps. *143*; 146 Hos. 5.8 – 6.6 1 Cor. 11. 2–16	Ps. *24*; 33 *alt.* Ps. *138*; 140; 141 Gen. ch. 15 Matt. 26. 47–56

Calendar and Holy Communion	Morning Prayer	Evening Prayer	NOTES

W or **G**	Amos ch. 9 1 Cor. 7. 25–end	Gen. 8.15 – 9.7 Matt. 25. 1–13	

Fabian, Bishop of Rome, Martyr, 250

Wr or **Gr**	Com. Martyr	Hos. 1.1 – 2.1 1 Cor. ch. 8	Gen. 9. 8–19 Matt. 25. 14–30

Agnes, Child Martyr at Rome, 304

Wr or **Gr**	Com. Virgin Martyr	Hos. 2. 2–17 1 Cor. 9. 1–14	Gen. 11. 1–9 Matt. 25. 31–end

ct

THE THIRD SUNDAY AFTER EPIPHANY

W or **G**	2 Kings 6. 14b–23 Ps. 102. 15–22 Rom. 12. 16b–end Matt. 8. 1–13	Ps. 113 Amos 3. 1–8 1 John 1. 1–4	Ps. 33 (or 33. 1–12) Eccles. 3. 1–11 1 Pet. 1. 3–12

W or **G**		Hos. 2.18 – 3.end 1 Cor. 9. 15–end	Gen. 11.27 – 12.9 Matt. 26. 1–16

W or **G**		Hos. 4. 1–16 1 Cor. 10. 1–13	Gen. 13. 2–end Matt. 26. 17–35 or First EP of The Conversion of Paul (Ps. 149) Isa. 49. 1–13 Acts 22. 3–16

W ct

THE CONVERSION OF PAUL

W	Josh. 5. 13–end Ps. 67 Acts 9. 1–22 Matt. 19. 27–end	(Ps. 66; 147. 13–end) Ezek. 3. 22–end Phil. 3. 1–14	(Ps. 119. 41–56) Ecclus. 39. 1–10 or Isa. 56. 1–8 Col. 1.24 – 2.7

W or **G**		Hos. 5.8 – 6.6 1 Cor. 11. 2–16	Gen. ch. 15 Matt. 26. 47–56

	Sunday Principal Service Weekday Eucharist	Third Service Morning Prayer	Second Service Evening Prayer

27 Friday

| W | Heb. 10. 32–end
Ps. 37. 3–6, 40–end
Mark 4. 26–34 | Ps. 61; *65*
alt. Ps. 142; *144*
Hos. 6.7 – 7.2
1 Cor. 11. 17–end | Ps. *67*; 77
alt. Ps. 145
Gen. ch. 16
Matt. 26. 57–end |

28 Saturday   Thomas Aquinas, Priest, Philosopher, Teacher, 1274

| W | Com. Teacher   *or*
esp. Wisd. 7. 7–10,
15–16
1 Cor. 2. 9–end
John 16. 12–15 | Heb. 11. 1–2, 8–19
Canticle: Luke 1. 69–73
Mark 4. 35–end | Ps. 68
alt. Ps. 147
Hos. ch. 8
1 Cor. 12. 1–11 | Ps. *72*; 76
alt. 148; 149; 150
Gen. 17. 1–22
Matt. 27. 1–10
ct |

29 Sunday   THE FOURTH SUNDAY OF EPIPHANY
or The Presentation of Christ in the Temple (Candlemas)*

| W | 1 Kings 17. 8–16
Ps. 36. 5–10
1 Cor. 1. 18–end
John 2. 1–11 | Ps. 71. 1–6, 15–17
Hag. 2. 1–9
1 Cor. 3. 10–17 | Ps. 34 (*or* 34. 1–10)
Gen. 28. 10–end
Philem. 1–16
Gospel: Mark 1. 21–28 |

30 Monday   Charles, King and Martyr, 1649
(Ordinary Time starts today if The Presentation is observed on 29 January)

| Wr [Gr]
DEL 4 | Com. Martyr   *or*
also Ecclus. 2. 12–17
1 Tim. 6. 12–16 | Heb. 11. 32–end
Ps. 31. 19–end
Mark 5. 1–20 | Ps. *57*; 96
alt. Ps. 1; 2; 3**
Hos. ch. 9
1 Cor. 12. 12–end | Ps. 2; *20*
alt. Ps. *4*; 7
Gen. 18. 1–15
Matt. 27. 11–26 |

31 Tuesday   *John Bosco, Priest, Founder of the Salesian Teaching Order, 1888*

| W | Heb. 12. 1–4
Ps. 22. 25b–end
Mark 5. 21–43 | Ps. *93*; 97
alt. Ps. *5*; 6; (8)
Hos. ch. 10
1 Cor. ch. 13 | Ps. *19*; 21
alt. Ps. 9; 10†
Gen. 18. 16–end
Matt. 27. 27–44 |

February 2023

1 Wednesday   *Brigid, Abbess of Kildare, c. 525*

| W | Heb. 12. 4–7, 11–15
Ps. 103. 1–2, 13–18
Mark 6. 1–6a | Ps. *95*; 98
alt. Ps. 119. 1–32
Hos. 11. 1–11
1 Cor. 14. 1–19 | *First EP of The*
Presentation
Ps. 118
1 Sam. 1. 19b–end
Heb. 4. 11–end
𝔚 **ct**
or, if The Presentation
is kept on 29 January:
Ps. *81*; 111
alt. Ps. *11*; 12; 13
Gen. 19. 1–3, 12–29
Matt. 27. 45–56 |

2 Thursday   THE PRESENTATION OF CHRIST IN THE TEMPLE (CANDLEMAS)

| 𝔴 | Mal. 3. 1–5
Ps. 24 (*or* 24. 7–end)
Heb. 2. 14–end
Luke 2. 22–40 | *MP:* Ps. *48*; 146
Exod. 13. 1–16
Rom. 12. 1–5 | *EP:* Ps. 122; *132*
Hag. 2. 1–9
John 2. 18–22 |

or, if The Presentation is observed on 29 January:

| G | Heb. 12. 18–19, 21–24
Ps. 48. 1–3, 8–10
Mark 6. 7–13 | Ps. 14; *15*; 16
Hos. 11.12 – 12.end
1 Cor. 14. 20–end | Ps. 18†
Gen. 21. 1–21
Matt. 27. 57–end |

*See provision for First EP on 1 February and throughout the day for The Presentation on 2 February.
**If The Presentation was observed on the 29 January, the alternative psalms are used this week.

Calendar and Holy Communion	Morning Prayer	Evening Prayer	NOTES
W or **G**	Hos. 6.7 – 7.2 1 Cor. 11. 17–end	Gen. ch. 16 Matt. 26. 57–end	
W or **G**	Hos. ch. 8 1 Cor. 12. 1–11	Gen. 17. 1–22 Matt. 27. 1–10 **ct**	

THE FOURTH SUNDAY AFTER THE EPIPHANY

W or **G**	1 Sam. 10. 17–24 Ps. 97 Rom. 13. 1–7 Matt. 8. 23–34	Ps. 71. 1–6, 15–17 Hag. 2. 1–9 1 Cor. 3. 10–17	Ps. 34 (or 34. 1–10) Gen. 28. 10–end Philem. 1–16	

Charles, King and Martyr, 1649

Wr or **Gr**	Com. Martyr	Hos. ch. 9 1 Cor. 12. 12–end	Gen. 18. 1–15 Matt. 27. 11–26	
W or **G**		Hos. ch. 10 1 Cor. ch. 13	Gen. 18. 16–end Matt. 27. 27–44	
W or **G**		Hos. 11. 1–11 1 Cor. 14. 1–19	*First EP of The Presentation* Ps. 118 1 Sam. 1. 19b–end Heb. 4. 11–end 𝔚 **ct**	

THE PRESENTATION OF CHRIST IN THE TEMPLE

𝔚	Mal. 3. 1–5 Ps. 48. 1–7 Gal. 4. 1–7 Luke 2. 22–40	Ps. 48; 146 Exod. 13. 1–16 Rom. 12. 1–5	Ps. 122; 132 Hag. 2. 1–9 John 2. 18–22	

		Sunday Principal Service Weekday Eucharist	Third Service Morning Prayer	Second Service Evening Prayer

3 Friday   **Anskar, Archbishop of Hamburg, Missionary in Denmark and Sweden, 865**
Ordinary Time starts today (or on 30 January if The Presentation is observed on 29 January)*

Gw	Com. Missionary *or*	Heb. 13. 1–8	Ps. 17; *19*	Ps. 22
	esp. Isa. 52. 7–10	Ps. 27. 1–6, 9–12	Hos. 13. 1–14	Gen. 22. 1–19
	also Rom. 10. 11–15	Mark 6. 14–29	1 Cor. 16. 1–9	Matt. 28. 1–15

4 Saturday   *Gilbert of Sempringham, Founder of the Gilbertine Order, 1189*

G		Heb. 13. 15–17, 20–21	Ps. 20; 21; *23*	Ps. *24*; 25
		Ps. 23	Hos. ch. 14	Gen. ch. 23
		Mark 6. 30–34	1 Cor. 16. 10–end	Matt. 28. 16–end
				ct

5 **Sunday**   **THE THIRD SUNDAY BEFORE LENT (Proper 1)**

G		Isa. 58. 1–9a [9b–12]	Ps. 5; 6	Ps. [1; 3] 4
		Ps. 112 (*or* 112. 1–9)	Jer. 26. 1–16	Amos 2. 4–end
		1 Cor. 2. 1–12 [13–end]	Acts 3. 1–10	Eph. 4. 17–end
		Matt. 5. 13–20		*Gospel*: Mark 1. 29–39

6 Monday   *The Martyrs of Japan, 1597*
(The Accession of Queen Elizabeth II may be observed on 6 February, and Collect, Readings and Post-Communion for the Sovereign used.)

G		Gen. 1. 1–19	Ps. 27; *30*	Ps. 26; *28*; 29
DEL 5		Ps. 104. 1–2, 6–13, 26	2 Chron. 2. 1–16	Gen. 24. 1–28
		Mark 6. 53–end	John 17. 1–5	1 Tim. 6. 1–10

7 Tuesday

G		Gen. 1.20 – 2.4a	Ps. 32; *36*	Ps. 33
		Ps. 8	2 Chron. ch. 3	Gen. 24. 29–end
		Mark 7. 1–13	John 17. 6–19	1 Tim. 6. 11–end

8 Wednesday

G		Gen. 2. 4b–9, 15–17	Ps. 34	Ps. 119. 33–56
		Ps. 104. 11–12, 29–32	2 Chron. ch. 5	Gen. 25. 7–11, 19–end
		Mark 7. 14–23	John 17. 20–end	2 Tim. 1. 1–14

9 Thursday

G		Gen. 2. 18–end	Ps. 37†	Ps. 39; *40*
		Ps. 128	2 Chron. 6. 1–21	Gen. 26.34 – 27.40
		Mark 7. 24–30	John 18. 1–11	2 Tim. 1.15 – 2.13

10 Friday   *Scholastica, sister of Benedict, Abbess of Plombariola, c. 543*

G		Gen. 3. 1–8	Ps. 31	Ps. 35
		Ps. 32. 1–8	2 Chron. 6. 22–end	Gen. 27.41 – 28.end
		Mark 7. 31–end	John 18. 12–27	2 Tim. 2. 14–end

11 Saturday

G		Gen. 3. 9–end	Ps. 41; *42*; 43	Ps. 45; *46*
		Ps. 90. 1–12	2 Chron. ch. 7	Gen. 29. 1–30
		Mark 8. 1–10	John 18. 28–end	2 Tim. ch. 3
				ct

12 **Sunday**   **THE SECOND SUNDAY BEFORE LENT**

G		Gen. 1.1 – 2.3	Ps. 100; 150	Ps. 148
		Ps. 136 (*or* 136. 1–9, 23–end)	Job 38. 1–21	Prov. 8. 1, 22–31
		Rom. 8. 18–25	Col. 1. 15–20	Rev. ch. 4
		Matt. 6. 25–end		*Gospel*: Luke 12. 16–31

*The Collect of 5 before Lent is used.

	Calendar and Holy Communion	Morning Prayer	Evening Prayer	NOTES
	Blasius, Bishop of Sebastopol, Martyr, c. 316			
Gr	Com. Martyr	Hos. 13. 1–14 1 Cor. 16. 1–9	Gen. 22. 1–19 Matt. 28. 1–15	
G		Hos. ch. 14 1 Cor. 16. 10–end	Gen. ch. 23 Matt. 28. 16–end	
			ct	
	SEPTUAGESIMA			
G	Gen. 1. 1–5 Ps. 9. 10–20 1 Cor. 9. 24–end Matt. 20. 1–16	Ps. 5; 6 Jer. 26. 1–16 Acts 3. 1–10	Ps. [1; 3] 4 Amos 2. 4–end Eph. 4. 17–end	
G	**The Accession of Queen Elizabeth II, 1952**			
	For Accession Service: Ps. 20; 101; 121; Josh. 1. 1–9; Prov. 8. 1–16; Rom. 13. 1–10; Rev. 21.22 - 22.4 *For The Accession:* 1 Pet. 2. 11–17 Matt. 22. 16–22	2 Chron. 2. 1–16 John 17. 1–5	Gen. 24. 1–28 1 Tim. 6. 1–10	
G		2 Chron. ch. 3 John 17. 6–19	Gen. 24. 29–end 1 Tim. 6. 11–end	
G		2 Chron. ch. 5 John 17. 20–end	Gen. 25. 7–11, 19–end 2 Tim. 1. 1–14	
G		2 Chron. 6. 1–21 John 18. 1–11	Gen. 26.34 - 27.40 2 Tim. 1.15 - 2.13	
G		2 Chron. 6. 22–end John 18. 12–27	Gen. 27.41 - 28.end 2 Tim. 2. 14–end	
G		2 Chron. ch. 7 John 18. 28–end	Gen. 29. 1–30 2 Tim. ch. 3	
			ct	
	SEXAGESIMA			
G	Gen. 3. 9–19 Ps. 83. 1–2, 13–end 2 Cor. 11. 19–31 Luke 8. 4–15	Ps. 100; 150 Job 38. 1–21 Col. 1. 15–20	Ps. 148 Prov. 8. 1, 22–31 Rev. ch. 4	

	Sunday Principal Service Weekday Eucharist	Third Service Morning Prayer	Second Service Evening Prayer

13 Monday

| G
DEL 6 | Gen. 4. 1–15, 25
Ps. 50. 1, 8, 16–end
Mark 8. 11–13 | Ps. 44
2 Chron. 9. 1–12
John 19. 1–16 | Ps. *47*; 49
Gen. 29.31 – 30.24
2 Tim. 4. 1–8 |

14 Tuesday **Cyril and Methodius, Missionaries to the Slavs, 869 and 885**
Valentine, Martyr at Rome, c. 269

| Gw | Com. Missionaries or Gen. 6. 5–8; 7. 1–5, 10
esp. Isa. 52. 7–10   Ps. 29
also Rom. 10. 11–15   Mark 8. 14–21 | Ps. *48*; 52
2 Chron. 10.1 – 11.4
John 19. 17–30 | Ps. 50
Gen. 31. 1–24
2 Tim. 4. 9–end |

15 Wednesday *Sigfrid, Bishop, Apostle of Sweden, 1045; Thomas Bray, Priest, Founder of the SPCK and SPG, 1730*

| G | Gen. 8. 6–13, 20–end
Ps. 116. 10–end
Mark 8. 22–26 | Ps. 119. 57–80
2 Chron. ch. 12
John 19. 31–end | Ps. *59*; 60; (67)
Gen. 31.25 – 32.2
Titus ch. 1 |

16 Thursday

| G | Gen. 9. 1–13
Ps. 102. 16–23
Mark 8. 27–33 | Ps. 56; *57*; (63†)
2 Chron. 13.1 – 14.1
John 20. 1–10 | 61; *62*; 64
Gen. 32. 3–30
Titus ch. 2 |

17 Friday **Janani Luwum, Archbishop of Uganda, Martyr, 1977**

| Gr | Com. Martyr   or Gen. 11. 1–9
also Ecclus. 4. 20–28 Ps. 33. 10–15
John 12. 24–32   Mark 8.34 – 9.1 | Ps. *51*; 54
2 Chron. 14. 2–end
John 20. 11–18 | Ps. 38
Gen. 33. 1–17
Titus ch. 3 |

18 Saturday

| G | Heb. 11. 1–7
Ps. 145. 1–10
Mark 9. 2–13 | Ps. 68
2 Chron. 15. 1–15
John 20. 19–end | Ps. 65; *66*
Gen. ch. 35
Philem.
ct |

19 Sunday **THE SUNDAY NEXT BEFORE LENT**

| G | Exod. 24. 12–end
Ps. 2
or Ps. 99
2 Pet. 1. 16–end
Matt. 17. 1–9 | Ps. 72
Exod. 34. 29–end
2 Cor. 4. 3–6 | Ps. 84
Ecclus. 48. 1–10
or 2 Kings 2. 1–12
Matt. 17. [1–8] 9–23 |

20 Monday

| G
DEL 7 | Ecclus. 1. 1–10
or James 1. 1–11
Ps. 93
or Ps. 119. 65–72
Mark 9. 14–29 | Ps. 71
Jer. ch. 1
John 3. 1–21 | Ps. *72*; 75
Gen. 37. 1–11
Gal. ch. 1 |

21 Tuesday

| G | Ecclus. 2. 1–11
or James 1. 12–18
Ps. 37. 3–6, 27–28
or Ps. 94. 12–18
Mark 9. 30–37 | Ps. 73
Jer. 2. 1–13
John 3. 22–end | Ps. 74
Gen. 37. 12–end
Gal. 2. 1–10 |

Calendar and Holy Communion		Morning Prayer	Evening Prayer	NOTES
G		2 Chron. 9. 1–12 John 19. 1–16	Gen. 29.31 – 30.24 2 Tim. 4. 1–8	
Valentine, Martyr at Rome, c. 269				
Gr	Com. Martyr	2 Chron. 10.1 – 11.4 John 19. 17–30	Gen. 31. 1–24 2 Tim. 4. 9–end	
G		2 Chron. ch. 12 John 19. 31–end	Gen. 31.25 – 32.2 Titus ch. 1	
G		2 Chron. 13.1 – 14.1 John 20. 1–10	Gen. 32. 3–30 Titus ch. 2	
G		2 Chron. 14. 2–end John 20. 11–18	Gen. 33. 1–17 Titus ch. 3	
G		2 Chron. 15. 1–15 John 20. 19–end	Gen. ch. 35 Philem.	
			ct	
QUINQUAGESIMA				
G	Gen. 9. 8–17 Ps. 77. 11–end 1 Cor. ch. 13 Luke 18. 31–43	Ps. 72 Exod. 34. 29–end 2 Cor. 4. 3–6	Ps. 84 Ecclus. 48. 1–10 or 2 Kings 2. 1–12 Matt. 17. [1–8] 9–23	
G		Jer. ch. 1 John 3. 1–21	Gen. 37. 1–11 Gal. ch. 1	
G		Jer. 2. 1–13 John 3. 22–end	Gen. 37. 12–end Gal. 2. 1–10	

	Sunday Principal Service / Weekday Eucharist	Third Service / Morning Prayer	Second Service / Evening Prayer

22 Wednesday **ASH WEDNESDAY**

P	Joel 2. 1–2, 12–17	*MP*: Ps. 38	*EP*: Ps. *51* or Ps. 102
	or Isa. 58. 1–12	Dan. 9. 3–6, 17–19	(or 102.1–18)
	Ps. 51. 1–18	1 Tim. 6. 6–19	Isa. 1. 10–18
	2 Cor. 5.20b – 6.10		Luke 15. 11–end
	Matt. 6. 1–6, 16–21		
	or John 8. 1–11		

23 Thursday   Polycarp, Bishop of Smyrna, Martyr, *c.* 155

Pr	Com. Martyr or	Deut. 30. 15–end	Ps. 77	Ps. 74
	also Rev. 2. 8–11	Ps. 1	*alt.* Ps. 78. 1–39†	*alt.* Ps. 78. 40–end†
		Luke 9. 22–25	Jer. 2. 14–32	Gen. ch. 39
			John 4. 1–26	Gal. 2. 11–end

24 Friday*

P	Isa. 58. 1–9a	Ps. *3*; 7	Ps. 31
	Ps. 51. 1–5, 17–18	*alt.* Ps. 55	*alt.* Ps. 69
	Matt. 9. 14–15	Jer. 3. 6–22	Gen. ch. 40
		John 4. 27–42	Gal. 3. 1–14

25 Saturday

P	Isa. 58. 9b–end	Ps. 71	Ps. 73
	Ps. 86. 1–7	*alt.* Ps. *76*; 79	*alt.* Ps. 81; *84*
	Luke 5. 27–32	Jer. 4. 1–18	Gen. 41. 1–24
		John 4. 43–end	Gal. 3. 15–22
			ct

26 Sunday   THE FIRST SUNDAY OF LENT

P	Gen. 2. 15–17; 3. 1–7	Ps. 119. 1–16	Ps. 50. 1–15
	Ps. 32	Jer. 18. 1–11	Deut. 6. 4–9, 16–end
	Rom. 5. 12–19	Luke 18. 9–14	Luke 15. 1–10
	Matt. 4. 1–11		

27 Monday   George Herbert, Priest, Poet, 1633

Pw	Com. Pastor or	Lev. 19. 1–2, 11–18	Ps. 10; *11*	Ps. 12; *13*; 14
	esp. Mal. 2. 5–7	Ps. 19. 7–end	*alt.* Ps. *80*; 82	*alt.* Ps. *85*; 86
	Matt. 11. 25–end	Matt. 25. 31–end	Jer. 4. 19–end	Gen. 41. 25–45
	also Rev. 19. 5–9		John 5. 1–18	Gal. 3.23 – 4.7

28 Tuesday

P	Isa. 55. 10–11	Ps. 44	Ps. 46; *49*
	Ps. 34. 4–6, 21–22	*alt.* Ps. 87; *89. 1–18*	*alt.* Ps. 89. 19–end
	Matt. 6. 7–15	Jer. 5. 1–19	Gen. 41.46 – 42.5
		John 5. 19–29	Gal. 4. 8–20

*Matthias may be celebrated on 24 February instead of 15 May.

Calendar and Holy Communion	Morning Prayer	Evening Prayer	NOTES

ASH WEDNESDAY

P	Ash Wednesday Collect until 8 April Commination Joel 2. 12–17 Ps. 57 James 4. 1–10 Matt. 6. 16–21	Ps. 38 Dan. 9. 3–6, 17–19 1 Tim. 6. 6–19	Ps. 51 *or* Ps. 102 (*or* 102. 1–18) Isa. 1. 10–18 Luke 15. 11–end	
P	Exod. 24. 12–end Matt. 8. 5–13	Jer. 2. 14–32 John 4. 1–26	Gen. ch. 39 Gal. 2. 11–end *or First EP of Matthias* (Ps. 147) Isa. 22. 15–22 Phil. 3.13b – 4.1 **R** ct	

MATTHIAS THE APOSTLE

R	1 Sam. 2. 27–35 Ps. 16. 1–7 Acts 1. 15–end Matt. 11. 25–end	(Ps. 15) Jonah 1. 1–9 Acts 2. 37–end	(Ps. 80) 1 Sam. 16. 1–13a Matt. 7. 15–27	
P	Isa. 38. 1–6a Mark 6. 45–end	Jer. 4. 1–18 John 4. 43–end	Gen. 41. 1–24 Gal. 3. 15–22 ct	

THE FIRST SUNDAY IN LENT

P	Collect (1) Lent 1 (2) Ash Wednesday Ember until 4 March Gen. 3. 1–6 Ps. 91. 1–12 2 Cor. 6. 1–10 Matt. 4. 1–11	Ps. 119. 1–16 Jer. 18. 1–11 Luke 18. 9–14	Ps. 50. 1–15 Deut. 6. 4–9, 16–end Luke 15. 1–10	
P	Ezek. 34. 11–16a Matt. 25. 31–end	Jer. 4. 19–end John 5. 1–18	Gen. 41. 25–45 Gal. 3.23 – 4.7	
P	Isa. 55. 6–11 Matt. 21. 10–16	Jer. 5. 1–19 John 5. 19–29	Gen. 41.46 – 42.5 Gal. 4. 8–20	

		Sunday Principal Service Weekday Eucharist	Third Service Morning Prayer	Second Service Evening Prayer

March 2023

1 Wednesday   **David, Bishop of Menevia, Patron of Wales, *c.* 601**
Ember Day*

Pw	Com. Bishop *or* *also* 2 Sam. 23. 1–4 Ps. 89. 19–22, 24	Jonah ch. 3 Ps. 51. 1–5, 17–18 Luke 11. 29–32	Ps. **6**; 17 *alt.* Ps. 119. 105–128 Jer. 5. 20–end John 5. 30–end	Ps. 9; **28** *alt.* Ps. **91**; 93 Gen. 42. 6–17 Gal. 4.21 – 5.1

2 Thursday   **Chad, Bishop of Lichfield, Missionary, 672****

Pw	Com. Missionary *or* *also* 1 Tim. 6. 11b–16	Esth. 14. 1–5, 12–14 *or* Isa. 55. 6–9 Ps. 138 Matt. 7. 7–12	Ps. **42**; 43 *alt.* Ps. 90; **92** Jer. 6. 9–21 John 6. 1–15	Ps. 137; 138; **142** *alt.* Ps. 94 Gen. 42. 18–28 Gal. 5. 2–15

3 Friday   Ember Day*

P		Ezek. 18. 21–28 Ps. 130 Matt. 5. 20–26	Ps. 22 *alt.* Ps. **88**; (95) Jer. 6. 22–end John 6. 16–27	Ps. 54; **55** *alt.* Ps. 102 Gen. 42. 29–end Gal. 5. 16–end

4 Saturday   Ember Day*

P		Deut. 26. 16–end Ps. 119. 1–8 Matt. 5. 43–end	Ps. 59; **63** *alt.* Ps. 96; **97**; 100 Jer. 7. 1–20 John 6. 27–40	Ps. **4**; 16 *alt.* Ps. 104 Gen. 43. 1–15 Gal. ch. 6 **ct**

5 **Sunday**   **THE SECOND SUNDAY OF LENT**

P		Gen. 12. 1–4a Ps. 121 Rom. 4. 1–5, 13–17 John 3. 1–17	Ps. 74 Jer. 22. 1–9 Matt. 8. 1–13	Ps. 135 (*or* 135. 1–14) Num. 21. 4–9 Luke 14. 27–33

6 Monday

P		Dan. 9. 4–10 Ps. 79. 8–9, 12, 14 Luke 6. 36–38	Ps. 26; **32** *alt.* Ps. **98**; 99; 101 Jer. 7. 21–end John 6. 41–51	Ps. 70; **74** *alt.* Ps. **105**† (*or* 103) Gen. 43. 16–end Heb. ch. 1

7 Tuesday   **Perpetua, Felicity and their Companions, Martyrs at Carthage, 203**

Pr	Com. Martyr *or* *esp.* Rev. 12. 10–12a *also* Wisd. 3. 1–7	Isa. 1. 10, 16–20 Ps. 50. 8, 16–end Matt. 23. 1–12	Ps. 50 *alt.* Ps. **106**† (*or* 103) Jer. 8. 1–15 John 6. 52–59	Ps. **52**; 53; 54 *alt.* Ps. 107† Gen. 44. 1–17 Heb. 2. 1–9

8 Wednesday   **Edward King, Bishop of Lincoln, 1910**
Felix, Bishop, Apostle to the East Angles, 647; Geoffrey Studdert Kennedy, Priest, Poet, 1929

Pw	Com. Bishop *or* *also* Heb. 13. 1–8	Jer. 18. 18–20 Ps. 31. 4–5, 14–18 Matt. 20. 17–28	Ps. 35 *alt.* Ps. 110; **111**; 112 Jer. 8.18 – 9.11 John 6. 60–end	Ps. **3**; 51 *alt.* Ps. 119. 129–152 Gen. 44. 18–end Heb. 2. 10–end

9 Thursday

P		Jer. 17. 5–10 Ps. 1 Luke 16. 19–end	Ps. 34 *alt.* Ps. 113; **115** Jer. 9. 12–24 John 7. 1–13	Ps. 71 *alt.* Ps. 114; **116**; 117 Gen. 45. 1–15 Heb. 3. 1–6

*For Ember Day provision, see p. 11.
**Chad may be celebrated with Cedd on 26 October instead of 2 March.

	Calendar and Holy Communion	Morning Prayer	Evening Prayer	NOTES

David, Bishop of Menevia, Patron of Wales, c. 601
Ember Day

Pw	Com. Bishop *or* Ember CEG *or* Isa. 58. 1–9a Matt. 12. 38–end	Jer. 5. 20–end John 5. 30–end	Gen. 42. 6–17 Gal. 4.21 – 5.1

Chad, Bishop of Lichfield, Missionary, 672

Pw	Com. Bishop *or* Isa. 58. 96–end John 8. 31–45	Jer. 6. 9–21 John 6. 1–15	Gen. 42. 18–28 Gal. 5. 2–15

Ember Day

P	Ember CEG *or* Ezek. 18. 20–25 John 5. 2–15	Jer. 6. 22–end John 6. 16–27	Gen. 42. 29–end Gal. 5. 16–end

Ember Day

P	Ember CEG *or* Ezek. 18. 26–end Matt. 17. 1–9 *or* Luke 4. 16–21 *or* John 10. 1–16	Jer. 7. 1–20 John 6. 27–40	Gen. 43. 1–15 Gal. ch. 6 **ct**

THE SECOND SUNDAY IN LENT

P	Jer. 17. 5–10 Ps. 25. 13–end 1 Thess. 4. 1–8 Matt. 15. 21–28	Ps. 74 Jer. 22. 1–9 Matt. 8. 1–13	Ps. 135 (*or* 135. 1–14) Num. 21. 4–9 Luke 14. 27–33

P	Heb. 2. 1–10 John 8. 21–30	Jer. 7. 21–end John 6. 41–51	Gen. 43. 16–end Heb. ch. 1

Perpetua, Martyr at Carthage, 203

Pr	Com. Martyr *or* Heb. 2. 11–end Matt. 23. 1–12	Jer. 8. 1–15 John 6. 52–59	Gen. 44. 1–17 Heb. 2. 1–9

P	Heb. 3. 1–6 Matt. 20. 17–28	Jer. 8.18 – 9.11 John 6. 60–end	Gen. 44. 18–end Heb. 2. 10–end

P	Heb. 3. 7–end John 5. 30–end	Jer. 9. 12–24 John 7. 1–13	Gen. 45. 1–15 Heb. 3. 1–6

		Sunday Principal Service Weekday Eucharist	Third Service Morning Prayer	Second Service Evening Prayer
10 Friday				
P		Gen. 37. 3–4, 12–13, 17–28 Ps. 105. 16–22 Matt. 21. 33–43, 45–46	Ps. 40; *41* *alt.* Ps. 139 Jer. 10. 1–16 John 7. 14–24	Ps. *6*; 38 *alt.* Ps. *130*; 131; 137 Gen. 45. 16–end Heb. 3. 7–end
11 Saturday				
P		Mic. 7. 4–15, 18–20 Ps. 103. 1–4, 9–12 Luke 15. 1–3, 11–end	Ps. 3; *25* *alt.* Ps. 120; *121*; 122 Jer. 10. 17–24 John 7. 25–36	Ps. *23*; 27 *alt.* Ps. 118 Gen. 46. 1–7, 28–end Heb. 4. 1–13 ct
12 Sunday	THE THIRD SUNDAY OF LENT			
P		Exod. 17. 1–7 Ps. 95 Rom. 5. 1–11 John 4. 5–42	Ps. 46 Amos 7. 10–end 2 Cor. 1. 1–11	Ps. 40 Josh. 1. 1–9 Eph. 6. 10–20 *Gospel:* John 2. 13–22
13 Monday*				
P		2 Kings 5. 1–15 Ps. 42. 1–2; 43. 1–4 Luke 4. 24–30	Ps. *5*; 7 *alt.* Ps. 123; 124; 125; *126* Jer. 11. 1–17 John 7. 37–52	Ps. 11; *17* *alt.* Ps. *127*; 128; 129 Gen. 47. 1–27 Heb. 4.14 – 5.10
14 Tuesday				
P		Song of the Three 2, 11–20 *or* Dan. 2. 20–23 Ps. 25. 3–10 Matt. 18. 21–end	Ps. 6; *9* *alt.* Ps. *132*; 133 Jer. 11.18 – 12.6 John 7.53 – 8.11	Ps. 61; 62; *64* *alt.* Ps. (134); *135* Gen. 47.28 – 48.end Heb. 5.11 – 6.12
15 Wednesday				
P		Deut. 4. 1, 5–9 Ps. 147. 13–end Matt. 5. 17–19	Ps. 38 *alt.* Ps. 119. 153–end Jer. 13. 1–11 John 8. 12–30	Ps. 36; *39* *alt.* Ps. 136 Gen. 49. 1–32 Heb. 6. 13–end
16 Thursday				
P		Jer. 7. 23–28 Ps. 95. 1–2, 6–end Luke 11. 14–23	Ps. *56*; 57 *alt.* Ps. *143*; 146 Jer. ch. 14 John 8. 31–47	Ps. *59*; 60 *alt.* Ps. *138*; 140; 141 Gen. 49.33 – 50.end Heb. 7. 1–10
17 Friday	Patrick, Bishop, Missionary, Patron of Ireland, *c.* 460			
Pw	Com. Missionary *or* *also* Ps. 91. 1–4, 13–end Luke 10. 1–12, 17–20	Hos. ch. 14 Ps. 81. 6–10, 13, 16 Mark 12. 28–34	Ps. 22 *alt.* Ps. 142; *144* Jer. 15. 10–end John 8. 48–end	Ps. 69 *alt.* Ps. 145 Exod. 1. 1–14 Heb. 7. 11–end
18 Saturday	*Cyril, Bishop of Jerusalem, Teacher, 386*			
P		Hos. 5.15 – 6.6 Ps. 51. 1–2, 17–end Luke 18. 9–14	Ps. 31 *alt.* Ps. 147 Jer. 16.10 – 17.4 John 9. 1–17	Ps. *116*; 130 *alt.* Ps. *148*; 149; 150 Exod. 1.22 – 2.10 Heb. ch. 8 ct

*The following readings may replace those provided for Holy Communion on any day during the Third Week of Lent: Exod. 17. 1–7; Ps. 95. 1–2, 6–end; John 4. 5–42.

	Calendar and Holy Communion	Morning Prayer	Evening Prayer	NOTES
P	Heb. ch. 4 Matt. 21. 33–end	Jer. 10. 1–16 John 7. 14–24	Gen. 45. 16–end Heb. 3. 7–end	
P	Heb. ch. 5 Luke 15. 11–end	Jer. 10. 17–24 John 7. 25–36	Gen. 46. 1–7, 28–end Heb. 4. 1–13	
			ct	
	THE THIRD SUNDAY IN LENT			
P	Num. 22. 21–31 Ps. 9. 13–end Eph. 5. 1–14 Luke 11. 14–28	Ps. 46 Amos 7. 10–end 2 Cor. 1. 1–11	Ps. 40 Josh. 1. 1–9 Eph. 6. 10–20	
P	Heb. 6. 1–10 Luke 4. 23–30	Jer. 11. 1–17 John 7. 37–52	Gen. 47. 1–27 Heb. 4.14 – 5.10	
P	Heb. 6. 11–end Matt. 18. 15–22	Jer. 11.18 – 12.6 John 7.53 – 8.11	Gen. 47.28 – 48.end Heb. 5.11 – 6.12	
P	Heb. 7. 1–10 Matt. 15. 1–20	Jer. 13. 1–11 John 8. 12–30	Gen. 49. 1–32 Heb. 6. 13–end	
P	Heb. 7. 11–25 John 6. 26–35	Jer. ch. 14 John 8. 31–47	Gen. 49.33 – 50.end Heb. 7. 1–10	
P	Heb. 7. 26–end John 4. 5–26	Jer. 15. 10–end John 8. 48–end	Exod. 1. 1–14 Heb. 7. 11–end	
	Edward, King of the West Saxons, 978			
Pr	Com. Martyr or Heb. 8. 1–6 John 8. 1–11	Jer. 16.10 – 17.4 John 9. 1–17	Exod. 1.22 – 2.10 Heb. ch. 8	
			ct	

		Sunday Principal Service Weekday Eucharist	Third Service Morning Prayer	Second Service Evening Prayer

19 Sunday   **THE FOURTH SUNDAY OF LENT** (Mothering Sunday)
              (Joseph transferred to 20 March)

P		1 Sam. 16. 1–13 Ps. 23 Eph. 5. 8–14 John ch. 9	Ps. 19 Isa. 43. 1–7 Eph. 2. 8–14	Ps. 31. 1–16 (*or* 31. 1–8) Mic. ch. 7 *or* Prayer of Manasseh James ch. 5 *Gospel:* John 3. 14–21 *or First EP of Joseph* Ps. 132 Hos. 11. 1–9 Luke 2. 41–end **W ct** *If the Principal Service readings for The Fourth Sunday of Lent are displaced by Mothering Sunday provisions, they may be used at the Second Service.*
	or, for Mothering Sunday:	Exod. 2. 1–10 *or* 1 Sam. 1. 20–end Ps. 34. 11–20 *or* Ps. 127. 1–4 2 Cor. 1. 3–7 *or* Col. 3. 12–17 Luke 2. 33–35 *or* John 19. 25b–27		

20 Monday*   **JOSEPH OF NAZARETH** (transferred from 19 March)**

W		2 Sam. 7. 4–16 Ps. 89. 26–36 Rom. 4. 13–18 Matt. 1. 18–end	*MP:* Ps. 25; 147. 1–12 Isa. 11. 1–10 Matt. 13. 54–end	*EP:* Ps. 1; 112 Gen. 50. 22–end Matt. 2. 13–end

21 Tuesday   Thomas Cranmer, Archbishop of Canterbury, Reformation Martyr, 1556

Pr	Com. Martyr	*or* Ezek. 47. 1–9, 12 Ps. 46. 1–8 John 5. 1–3, 5–16	Ps. 54; **79** *alt.* Ps. 5; 6; (8) Jer. 18. 1–12 John 10. 1–10	Ps. **80**; 82 *alt.* Ps. **9**; 10† Exod. 2.23 – 3.20 Heb. 9. 15–end

22 Wednesday

P		Isa. 49. 8–15 Ps. 145. 8–18 John 5. 17–30	Ps. **63**; 90 *alt.* Ps. 119. 1–32 Jer. 18. 13–end John 10. 11–21	Ps. 52; **91** *alt.* Ps. **11**; 12; 13 Exod. 4. 1–23 Heb. 10. 1–18

23 Thursday

P		Exod. 32. 7–14 Ps. 106. 19–23 John 5. 31–end	Ps. 53; **86** *alt.* Ps. 14; **15**; 16 Jer. 19. 1–13 John 10. 22–end	Ps. 94 *alt.* Ps. 18† Exod. 4.27 – 6.1 Heb. 10. 19–25

*The following readings may replace those provided for Holy Communion on any day (except Joseph of Nazareth and The Annunciation) during the Fourth Week of Lent: Mic. 7. 7–9; Ps. 27. 1, 9–10, 16–17; John ch. 9.
**Cuthbert may be celebrated on 4 September.

Calendar and Holy Communion	Morning Prayer	Evening Prayer	NOTES

THE FOURTH SUNDAY IN LENT
To celebrate Mothering Sunday, see *Common Worship* provision.

P	Exod. 16. 2–7a	Ps. 19	Ps. 31. 1–16 (*or* 31. 1–8)
	Ps. 122	Isa. 43. 1–7	Mic. ch. 7
	Gal. 4. 21–end	Eph. 2. 8–14	*or* Prayer of Manasseh
	or Heb. 12. 22–24		James ch. 5
	John 6. 1–14		

To celebrate Joseph, see *Common Worship* provision.

P	Heb. 11. 1–6	Jer. 17. 5–18	Exod. 2. 11–22
	John 2. 13–end	John 9. 18–end	Heb. 9. 1–14

Benedict, Abbot of Monte Cassino, c. 550

Pw	Com. Abbot *or*	Jer. 18. 1–12	Exod. 2.23 – 3.20
	Heb. 11. 13–16a	John 10. 1–10	Heb. 9. 15–end
	John 7. 14–24		

P	Heb. 12. 1–11	Jer. 18. 13–end	Exod. 4. 1–23
	John 9. 1–17	John 10. 11–21	Heb. 10. 1–18

P	Heb. 12. 12–17	Jer. 19. 1–13	Exod. 4.27 – 6.1
	John 5. 17–27	John 10. 22–end	Heb. 10. 19–25

		Sunday Principal Service Weekday Eucharist	Third Service Morning Prayer	Second Service Evening Prayer
24 Friday		*Walter Hilton of Thurgarton, Augustinian Canon, Mystic, 1396; Paul Couturier, Priest, Ecumenist, 1953; Oscar Romero, Archbishop of San Salvador, Martyr, 1980*		
P		Wisd. 2. 1, 12–22 or Jer. 26. 8–11 Ps. 34. 15–end John 7. 1–2, 10, 25–30	Ps. 102 *alt.* Ps. 17; *19* Jer. 19.14 – 20.6 John 11. 1–16	*First EP of The Annunciation* Ps. 85 Wisd. 9. 1–12 or Gen. 3. 8–15 Gal. 4. 1–5 𝔴 ct
25 Saturday	**THE ANNUNCIATION OF OUR LORD TO THE BLESSED VIRGIN MARY**			
𝔴		Isa. 7. 10–14 Ps. 40. 5–11 Heb. 10. 4–10 Luke 1. 26–38	*MP*: Ps. 111; 113 1 Sam. 2. 1–10 Rom. 5. 12–end	*EP*: Ps. 131; 146 Isa. 52. 1–12 Heb. 2. 5–end
26 Sunday	**THE FIFTH SUNDAY OF LENT (Passiontide begins)**			
P		Ezek. 37. 1–14 Ps. 130 Rom. 8. 6–11 John 11. 1–45	Ps. 86 Jer. 31. 27–37 John 12. 20–33	Ps. 30 Lam. 3. 19–33 Matt. 20. 17–end
27 Monday*				
P		Susanna 1–9, 15–17, 19–30, 33–62 (or 41b–62) or Josh. 2. 1–14 Ps. 23 John 8. 1–11	Ps. *73*; 121 *alt.* Ps. 27; *30* Jer. 21. 1–10 John 11. 28–44	Ps. *26*; 27 *alt.* Ps. 26; *28*; 29 Exod. 8. 1–19 Heb. 11. 17–31
28 Tuesday				
P		Num. 21. 4–9 Ps. 102. 1–3, 16–23 John 8. 21–30	Ps. *35*; 123 *alt.* Ps. 32; *36* Jer. 22. 1–5, 13–19 John 11. 45–end	Ps. *61*; 64 *alt.* Ps. 33 Exod. 8. 20–end Heb. 11.32 – 12.2
29 Wednesday				
P		Dan. 3. 14–20, 24–25, 28 *Canticle*: Bless the Lord John 8. 31–42	Ps. *55*; 124 *alt.* Ps. 34 Jer. 22.20 – 23.8 John 12. 1–11	Ps. 56; *62* *alt.* Ps. 119. 33–56 Exod. 9. 1–12 Heb. 12. 3–13
30 Thursday				
P		Gen. 17. 3–9 Ps. 105. 4–9 John 8. 51–end	Ps. *40*; 125 *alt.* Ps. 37† Jer. 23. 9–32 John 12. 12–19	Ps. 42; *43* *alt.* Ps. 39; *40* Exod. 9. 13–end Heb. 12. 14–end
31 Friday	*John Donne, Priest, Poet, 1631*			
P		Jer. 20. 10–13 Ps. 18. 1–6 John 10. 31–end	Ps. *22*; 126 *alt.* Ps. 31 Jer. ch. 24 John 12. 20–36a	Ps. 31 *alt.* Ps. 35 Exod. ch. 10 Heb. 13. 1–16

*The following readings may replace those provided for Holy Communion on any day during the Fifth Week of Lent: 2 Kings 4. 18–21, 32–37; Ps. 17. 1–8, 16; John 11. 1–45.

Calendar and Holy Communion	Morning Prayer	Evening Prayer	NOTES

| P | Heb. 12. 22–end
John 11. 33–46 | | *First EP of The*
Annunciation
Ps. 85
Wisd. 9. 1–12
or Gen. 3. 8–15
Gal. 4. 1–5
𝔴 ct | |

THE ANNUNCIATION OF THE BLESSED VIRGIN MARY

| 𝔴 | Isa. 7. 10–14 [15]
Ps. 113
Rom. 5. 12–19
Luke 1. 26–38 | Ps. 111
1 Sam. 2. 1–10
Heb. 10. 4–10 | Ps. 131; 146
Isa. 52. 1–12
Heb. 2. 5–end | |

THE FIFTH SUNDAY IN LENT

| P | Exod. 24. 4–8
Ps. 143
Heb. 9. 11–15
John 8. 46–end | Ps. 86
Jer. 31. 27–37
John 12. 20–33 | Ps. 30
Lam. 3. 19–33
Matt. 20. 17–end | |

| P | Col. 1. 13–23a
John 7. 1–13 | Jer. 21. 1–10
John 11. 28–44 | Exod. 8. 1–19
Heb. 11. 17–31 | |

| P | Col. 2. 8–12
John 7. 32–39 | Jer. 22. 1–5, 13–19
John 11. 45–end | Exod. 8. 20–end
Heb. 11.32 – 12.2 | |

| P | Col. 2. 13–19
John 7. 40–end | Jer. 22.20 – 23.8
John 12. 1–11 | Exod. 9. 1–12
Heb. 12. 3–13 | |

| P | Col. 3. 8–11
John 10. 22–38 | Jer. 23. 9–32
John 12. 12–19 | Exod. 9. 13–end
Heb. 12. 14–end | |

| P | Col. 3. 12–17
John 11. 47–54 | Jer. ch. 24
John 12. 20–36a | Exod. ch. 10
Heb. 13. 1–16 | |

	Sunday Principal Service Weekday Eucharist	Third Service Morning Prayer	Second Service Evening Prayer

April 2023

1 Saturday   *Frederick Denison Maurice, Priest, Teacher, 1872*

P	Ezek. 37. 21–end Canticle: Jer. 31. 10–13 or Ps. 121 John 11. 45–end	Ps. *23*; 127 alt. Ps. 41; *42*; 43 Jer. 25. 1–14 John 12. 36b–end	Ps. 128; 129; *130* alt. Ps. 45; *46* Exod. ch. 11 Heb. 13. 17–end ct

2 Sunday   **PALM SUNDAY**

R	*Liturgy of the Palms* Matt. 21. 1–11 Ps. 118. 1–2, 19–end (or 118. 19–24) *Liturgy of the Passion* Isa. 50. 4–9a Ps. 31. 9–16 (or 31. 9–18) Phil. 2. 5–11 Matt. 26.14 – 27.end or Matt. 27. 11–54	Ps. 61; 62 Zech. 9. 9–12 Luke 16. 19–end	Ps. 80 Isa. 5. 1–7 Matt. 21. 33–end

3 Monday   **MONDAY OF HOLY WEEK**

R	Isa. 42. 1–9 Ps. 36. 5–11 Heb. 9. 11–15 John 12. 1–11	*MP*: Ps. 41 Lam. 1. 1–12a Luke 22. 1–23	*EP*: Ps. 25 Lam. 2. 8–19 Col. 1. 18–23

4 Tuesday   **TUESDAY OF HOLY WEEK**

R	Isa. 49. 1–7 Ps. 71. 1–8 [9–14] 1 Cor. 1. 18–31 John 12. 20–36	*MP*: Ps. 27 Lam. 3. 1–18 Luke 22. [24–38] 39–53	*EP*: Ps. 55. 13–24 Lam. 3. 40–51 Gal. 6. 11–end

5 Wednesday   **WEDNESDAY OF HOLY WEEK**

R	Isa. 50. 4–9a Ps. 70 Heb. 12. 1–3 John 13. 21–32	*MP*: Ps. 102 (or 102. 1–8) Wisd. 1.16 – 2.1, 12–22 or Jer. 11. 18–20 Luke 22. 54–end	*EP*: Ps. 88 Isa. 63. 1–9 Rev. 14.18 – 15.4

6 Thursday   **MAUNDY THURSDAY**

W (HC) R	Exod. 12. 1–4 [5–10], 11–14 Ps. 116. 1, 10–end (or 116. 9–end) 1 Cor. 11. 23–26 John 13. 1–17, 31b–35	*MP*: Ps. 42; 43 Lev. 16. 2–24 Luke 23. 1–25	*EP*: Ps. 39 Exod. ch. 11 Eph. 2. 11–18

7 Friday   **GOOD FRIDAY**

R	Isa. 52.13 – 53.end Ps. 22 (or 22. 1–11 or 22. 1–21) Heb. 10. 16–25 or Heb. 10. 14–16; 5. 7–9 John 18.1 – 19.end	*MP*: Ps. 69 Gen. 22. 1–18 *A part of* John 18 – 19 *if not read at the Principal Service* or Heb. 10. 1–10	*EP*: Ps. 130; 143 Lam. 5. 15–end *A part of* John 18 – 19 *if not read at the Principal Service, especially* John 19. 38–end or Col. 1. 18–23

Calendar and Holy Communion	Morning Prayer	Evening Prayer	NOTES

P Col. 4. 2–6 John 6. 53–end	Jer. 25. 1–14 John 12. 36b–end	Exod. ch. 11 Heb. 13. 17–end	

ct

THE SUNDAY NEXT BEFORE EASTER (PALM SUNDAY)

R Zech. 9. 9–12 Ps. 73. 22–end Phil. 2. 5–11 Passion according to Matthew Matt. 27. 1–54 *or* Matt. 26.1 – 27.61 *or* Matt. 21. 1–13	Ps. 61; 62 Isa. 42. 1–9 Luke 16. 19–end	Ps. 80 Isa. 5. 1–7 Matt. 21. 33–end	

MONDAY IN HOLY WEEK

R Isa. 63. 1–19 Ps. 55. 1–8 Gal. 6. 1–11 Mark ch. 14	Ps. 41 Lam. 1. 1–12a John 12. 1–11	Ps. 25 Lam. 2. 8–19 Col. 1. 18–23	

TUESDAY IN HOLY WEEK

R Isa. 50. 5–11 Ps. 13 Rom. 5. 6–19 Mark 15. 1–39	Ps. 27 Lam. 3. 1–18 John 12. 20–36	Ps. 55. 13–24 Lam. 3. 40–51 Gal. 6. 11–end	

WEDNESDAY IN HOLY WEEK

R Isa. 49. 1–9a Ps. 54 Heb. 9. 16–end Luke ch. 22	Ps. 102 (*or* 102. 1–8) Wisd. 1.16 – 2.1, 12–22 *or* Jer. 11. 18–20 John 13. 21–32	Ps. 88 Isa. 63. 1–9 Rev. 14.18 – 15.4	

MAUNDY THURSDAY

W Exod. 12. 1–11 **(HC)** Ps. 43 **R** 1 Cor. 11. 17–end Luke 23. 1–49	Ps. 42; 43 Lev. 16. 2–24 John 13. 1–17, 31b–35	Ps. 39 Exod. ch. 11 Eph. 2. 11–18	

GOOD FRIDAY

R Alt. Collect Passion according to John Alt. Gospel, if Passion is read Num. 21. 4–9 Ps. 140. 1–9 Heb. 10. 1–25 John 19. 1–37 *or* John 19. 38–end	Ps. 69 Gen. 22. 1–18 John ch. 18	Ps. 130; 143 Lam. 5. 15–end John 19. 38–end	

		Sunday Principal Service Weekday Eucharist	Third Service Morning Prayer	Second Service Evening Prayer
8 Saturday	**EASTER EVE**			
	These readings are for use at services other than the Easter Vigil.	Job 14. 1–14 or Lam. 3. 1–9, 19–24 Ps. 31. 1–4, 15–16 (or 31. 1–5) 1 Pet. 4. 1–8 Matt. 27. 57–end or John 19. 38–end	Ps. 142 Hos. 6. 1–6 John 2. 18–22	Ps. 116 Job 19. 21–27 1 John 5. 5–12
9 Sunday	**EASTER DAY**			
w	*The following readings and psalms (or canticles) are provided for use at the Easter Vigil. A minimum of three Old Testament readings should be chosen. The reading from Exodus ch. 14 should always be used.*	Gen. 1.1 – 2.4a & Ps. 136. 1–9, 23–end Gen. 7. 1–5, 11–18; 8. 6–18; 9. 8–13 & Ps. 46 Gen. 22. 1–18 & Ps. 16 Exod. 14. 10–end; 15. 20–21 & *Canticle*: Exod. 15. 1b–13, 17–18 Isa. 55. 1–11 & *Canticle*: Isa. 12. 2–end Baruch 3.9–15, 32 – 4.4 & Ps. 19 *or* Prov. 8. 1–8, 19–21; 9. 4b–6 & Ps. 19 Ezek. 36. 24–28 & Ps. 42; 43 Ezek. 37. 1–14 & Ps. 143 Zeph. 3. 14–end & Ps. 98 Rom. 6. 3–11 & Ps. 114 Matt. 28. 1–10		
w	*Easter Day Services The reading from Acts must be used as either the first or second reading at the Principal Service.*	Acts 10. 34–43 or Jer. 31. 1–6 Ps. 118. 1–2, 14–24 (or 118. 14–24) Col. 3. 1–4 or Acts 10. 34–43 John 20. 1–18 or Matt. 28. 1–10	*MP*: Ps. 114; 117 Exod. 14.10–18, 26 – 15.2 Rev. 15. 2–4	*EP*: Ps. 105 or Ps. 66. 1–11 Song of Sol. 3. 2–5; 8. 6–7 John 20. 11–18 *if not used at the Principal Service* or Rev. 1. 12–18
10 Monday	**MONDAY OF EASTER WEEK**			
W		Acts 2. 14, 22–32 Ps. 16. 1–2, 6–end Matt. 28. 8–15	Ps. *111*; 117; 146 Song of Sol. 1.9 – 2.7 Mark 16. 1–8	Ps. 135 Exod. 12. 1–14 1 Cor. 15. 1–11
11 Tuesday	**TUESDAY OF EASTER WEEK**			
W		Acts 2. 36–41 Ps. 33. 4–5, 18–end John 20. 11–18	Ps. *112*; 147. 1–12 Song of Sol. 2. 8–end Luke 24. 1–12	Ps. 136 Exod. 12. 14–36 1 Cor. 15. 12–19
12 Wednesday	**WEDNESDAY OF EASTER WEEK**			
W		Acts 3. 1–10 Ps. 105. 1–9 Luke 24. 13–35	Ps. *113*; 147. 13–end Song of Sol. ch. 3 Matt. 28. 16–end	Ps. 105 Exod. 12. 37–end 1 Cor. 15. 20–28
13 Thursday	**THURSDAY OF EASTER WEEK**			
W		Acts 3. 11–end Ps. 8 Luke 24. 35–48	Ps. *114*; 148 Song of Sol. 5.2 – 6.3 Luke 7. 11–17	Ps. 106 Exod. 13. 1–16 1 Cor. 15. 29–34
14 Friday	**FRIDAY OF EASTER WEEK**			
W		Acts 4. 1–12 Ps. 118. 1–4, 22–26 John 21. 1–14	Ps. *115*; 149 Song of Sol. 7.10 – 8.4 Luke 8. 41–end	Ps. 107 Exod. 13.17 – 14.14 1 Cor. 15. 35–50

Calendar and Holy Communion	Morning Prayer	Evening Prayer	NOTES
EASTER EVE			
Job 14. 1–14 1 Pet. 3. 17–22 Matt. 27. 57–end	Ps. 142 Hos. 6. 1–6 John 2. 18–22	Ps. 116 Job 19. 21–27 1 John 5. 5–12	
EASTER DAY			
ℬ Exod. 12. 21–28 Ps. 111 Col. 3. 1–7 John 20. 1–10	Ps. 114; 117 Exod. 14.10–18, 26 – 15.2 Rev. 15. 2–4	Ps. 105 or Ps. 66. 1–11 Song of Sol. 3. 2–5; 8. 6–7 John 20. 11–18 or Rev. 1. 12–18	
MONDAY IN EASTER WEEK			
W Hos. 6. 1–6 Easter Anthems Acts 10. 34–43 Luke 24. 13–35	Song of Sol. 1.9 – 2.7 Mark 16. 1–8	Exod. 12. 1–14 1 Cor. 15. 1–11	
TUESDAY IN EASTER WEEK			
W 1 Kings 17. 17–end Ps. 16. 9–end Acts 13. 26–41 Luke 24. 36b–48	Song of Sol. 2. 8–end Luke 24. 1–12	Exod. 12. 14–36 1 Cor. 15. 12–19	
W Isa. 42. 10–16 Ps. 111 Acts 3. 12–18 John 20. 11–18	Song of Sol. ch. 3 Matt. 28. 16–end	Exod. 12. 37–end 1 Cor. 15. 20–28	
W Isa. 43. 16–21 Ps. 113 Acts 8. 26–end John 21. 1–14	Song of Sol. 5.2 – 6.3 Luke 7. 11–17	Exod. 13. 1–16 1 Cor. 15. 29–34	
W Ezek. 37. 1–14 Ps. 116. 1–9 1 Pet. 3. 18–end Matt. 28. 16–end	Song of Sol. 7.10 – 8.4 Luke 8. 41–end	Exod. 13.17 – 14.14 1 Cor. 15. 35–50	

		Sunday Principal Service Weekday Eucharist	Third Service Morning Prayer	Second Service Evening Prayer
15 Saturday	**SATURDAY OF EASTER WEEK**			
W		Acts 4. 13–21 Ps. 118. 1–4, 14–21 Mark 16. 9–15	Ps. *116*; 150 Song of Sol. 8. 5–7 John 11. 17–44	Ps. 145 Exod. 14. 15–end 1 Cor. 15. 51–end **ct**
16 Sunday	**THE SECOND SUNDAY OF EASTER**			
W	*The reading from Acts must be used as either the first or second reading at the Principal Service.*	Acts 2. 14a, 22–32 [or Exod. 14. 10–end; 15. 20–21] Ps. 16 1 Pet. 1. 3–9 John 20. 19–end	Ps. 81. 1–10 Exod. 12. 1–17 1 Cor. 5. 6b–8	Ps. 30. 1–5 Dan. 6. [1–5] 6–23 Mark 15.46 – 16.8
17 Monday				
W		Acts 4. 23–31 Ps. 2. 1–9 John 3. 1–8	Ps. 2; *19* *alt.* Ps. *1*; 2; 3 Deut. 1. 3–18 John 20. 1–10	Ps. 139 *alt.* Ps. *4*; 7 Exod. 15. 1–21 Col. 1. 1–14
18 Tuesday				
W		Acts 4. 32–end Ps. 93 John 3. 7–15	Ps. *8*; 20; 21 *alt.* Ps. *5*; 6; (8) Deut. 1. 19–40 John 20. 11–18	Ps. 104 *alt.* Ps. *9*; 10† Exod. 15.22 – 16.10 Col. 1. 15–end
19 Wednesday	Alphege, Archbishop of Canterbury, Martyr, 1012			
Wr	Com. Martyr or *also* Heb. 5. 1–4	Acts 5. 17–26 Ps. 34. 1–8 John 3. 16–21	Ps. 16; *30* *alt.* Ps. 119. 1–32 Deut. 3. 18–end John 20. 19–end	Ps. 33 *alt.* Ps. *11*; 12; 13 Exod. 16. 11–end Col. 2. 1–15
20 Thursday				
W		Acts 5. 27–33 Ps. 34. 1, 15–end John 3. 31–end	Ps. *28*; 29 *alt.* Ps. 14; *15*; 16 Deut. 4. 1–14 John 21. 1–14	Ps. 34 *alt.* Ps. 18† Exod. ch. 17 Col. 2.16 – 3.11
21 Friday	Anselm, Abbot of Le Bec, Archbishop of Canterbury, Teacher, 1109			
W	Com. Teacher or *also* Wisd. 9. 13–end Rom. 5. 8–11	Acts 5. 34–42 Ps. 27. 1–5, 16–17 John 6. 1–15	Ps. 57; *61* *alt.* Ps. 17; *19* Deut. 4. 15–31 John 21. 15–19	Ps. 118 *alt.* Ps. 22 Exod. 18. 1–12 Col. 3.12 – 4.1
22 Saturday				
W		Acts 6. 1–7 Ps. 33. 1–5, 18–19 John 6. 16–21	Ps. 63; *84* *alt.* Ps. 20; 21; *23* Deut. 4. 32–40 John 21. 20–end	Ps. 66 *alt.* Ps. *24*; 25 Exod. 18. 13–end Col. 4. 2–end **ct**

Calendar and Holy Communion	Morning Prayer	Evening Prayer	NOTES
W Zech. 8. 1–8 Ps. 118. 14–21 1 Pet. 2. 1–10 John 20. 24–end	Song of Sol. 8. 5–7 John 11. 17–44	Exod. 14. 15–end 1 Cor. 15. 51–end **ct**	
THE FIRST SUNDAY AFTER EASTER			
W Ezek. 37. 1–10 Ps. 81. 1–4 1 John 5. 4–12 John 20. 19–23	Ps. 81. 1–10 Exod. 12. 1–17 1 Cor. 5. 6b–8	Ps. 30. 1–5 Dan. 6. [1–5] 6–23 Mark 15.46 – 16.8	
W	Deut. 1. 3–18 John 20. 1–10	Exod. 15. 1–21 Col. 1. 1–14	
W	Deut. 1. 19–40 John 20. 11–18	Exod. 15.22 – 16.10 Col. 1. 15–end	
Alphege, Archbishop of Canterbury, Martyr, 1012			
Wr Com. Martyr	Deut. 3. 18–end John 20. 19–end	Exod. 16. 11–end Col. 2. 1–15	
W	Deut. 4. 1–14 John 21. 1–14	Exod. ch. 17 Col. 2.16 – 3.11	
W	Deut. 4. 15–31 John 21. 15–19	Exod. 18. 1–12 Col. 3.12 – 4.1	
W	Deut. 4. 32–40 John 21. 20–end	Exod. 18. 13–end Col. 4. 2–end **ct**	

	Sunday Principal Service / Weekday Eucharist	Third Service / Morning Prayer	Second Service / Evening Prayer
23 Sunday	**THE THIRD SUNDAY OF EASTER** (George transferred to 24 April)		
W	*The reading from Acts must be used as either the first or second reading at the Principal Service.* Acts 2. 14a, 36–41 [or Zeph. 3. 14–end] Ps. 116. 1–3, 10–end (or 116. 1–7) 1 Pet. 1. 17–23 Luke 24. 13–35	Ps. 23 Isa. 40. 1–11 1 Pet. 5. 1–11	Ps. 48 Hag. 1.13 – 2.9 1 Cor. 3. 10–17 *Gospel:* John 2. 13–22 *or First EP of George* Ps. 111; 116 Jer. 15. 15–end Heb. 11.32 – 12.2 **R ct**
24 Monday	**GEORGE, MARTYR, PATRON OF ENGLAND, c. 304** (transferred from 23 April)		
R	1 Macc. 2. 59–64 or Rev. 12. 7–12 Ps. 126 2 Tim. 2. 3–13 John 15. 18–21	*MP*: Ps. 5; 146 Josh. 1. 1–9 Eph. 6. 10–20	*EP*: Ps. 3; 11 Isa. 43. 1–7 John 15. 1–8 *or First EP of Mark* Ps. 19 Isa. 52. 7–10 Mark 1. 1–15 **R ct**
25 Tuesday	**MARK THE EVANGELIST**		
R	Prov. 15. 28–end or Acts 15. 35–end Ps. 119. 9–16 Eph. 4. 7–16 Mark 13. 5–13	*MP*: Ps. 37. 23–end; 148 Isa. 62. 6–10 or Ecclus. 51. 13–end Acts 12.25 – 13.13	*EP*: Ps. 45 Ezek. 1. 4–14 2 Tim. 4. 1–11
26 Wednesday			
W	Acts 8. 1b–8 Ps. 66. 1–6 John 6. 35–40	Ps. 105 *alt.* Ps. 34 Deut. ch. 6 Eph. 2. 1–10	Ps. 67; *72* *alt.* Ps. 119. 33–56 Exod. ch. 24 Luke 1. 39–56
27 Thursday	*Christina Rossetti, Poet, 1894*		
W	Acts 8. 26–end Ps. 66. 7–8, 14–end John 6. 44–51	Ps. 136 *alt.* Ps. 37† Deut. 7. 1–11 Eph. 2. 11–end	Ps. 73 *alt.* Ps. 39; *40* Exod. 25. 1–22 Luke 1. 57–end
28 Friday	*Peter Chanel, Missionary in the South Pacific, Martyr, 1841*		
W	Acts 9. 1–20 Ps. 117 John 6. 52–59	Ps. 107 *alt.* Ps. 31 Deut. 7. 12–end Eph. 3. 1–13	Ps. 77 *alt.* Ps. 35 Exod. 28. 1–4a, 29–38 Luke 2. 1–20
29 Saturday	*Catherine of Siena, Teacher, 1380*		
W	Com. Teacher or *also* Prov. 8. 1, 6–11 John 17. 12–end Acts 9. 31–42 Ps. 116. 10–15 John 6. 60–69	Ps. 108; *110*; 111 *alt.* Ps. 41; *42*; 43 Deut. ch. 8 Eph. 3. 14–end	Ps. 23; *27* *alt.* Ps. 45; *46* Exod. 29. 1–9 Luke 2. 21–40 **ct**

Calendar and Holy Communion	Morning Prayer	Evening Prayer	NOTES
THE SECOND SUNDAY AFTER EASTER (George transferred to 24 April)			
W Ezek. 34. 11–16a Ps. 23 1 Pet. 2. 19–end John 10. 11–16	Ps. 23 Isa. 40. 1–11 1 Pet. 5. 1–11	Ps. 48 Hag. 1.13 – 2.9 1 Cor. 3. 10–17	
George, Martyr, Patron of England, c. 304 To celebrate George, see *Common Worship* provision.			
Wr Com. Martyr	Deut. 5. 1–22 Eph. 1. 1–14	Exod. ch. 19 Luke 1. 1–25 *or First EP of Mark* (Ps. 19) Isa. 52. 7–10 Mark 1. 1–15	
		R ct	
MARK THE EVANGELIST			
R Prov. 15. 28–end Ps. 119. 9–16 Eph. 4. 7–16 John 15. 1–11	(Ps. 37. 23–end; 148) Isa. 62. 6–10 *or* Ecclus. 51. 13–end Acts 12.25 – 13.13	(Ps. 45) Ezek. 1. 4–14 2 Tim. 4. 1–11	
W	Deut. ch. 6 Eph. 2. 1–10	Exod. ch. 24 Luke 1. 39–56	
W	Deut. 7. 1–11 Eph. 2. 11–end	Exod. 25. 1–22 Luke 1. 57–end	
W	Deut. 7. 12–end Eph. 3. 1–13	Exod. 28. 1–4a, 29–38 Luke 2. 1–20	
W	Deut. ch. 8 Eph. 3. 14–end	Exod. 29. 1–9 Luke 2. 21–40	
		ct	

	Sunday Principal Service Weekday Eucharist	Third Service Morning Prayer	Second Service Evening Prayer

30 Sunday   THE FOURTH SUNDAY OF EASTER

| W | *The reading from Acts must be used as either the first or second reading at the Principal Service.* | Acts 2. 42–end
[*or* Gen. ch. 7]
Ps. 23
1 Pet. 2. 19–end
John 10. 1–10 | Ps. 106. 6–24
Neh. 9. 6–15
1 Cor. 10. 1–13 | Ps. 29. 1–10
Ezra 3. 1–13
Eph. 2. 11–end
Gospel: Luke 19. 37–end
or First EP of Philip and James
Ps. 25
Isa. 40. 27–end
John 12. 20–26
R ct |

May 2023

1 Monday   PHILIP AND JAMES, APOSTLES

| R | | Isa. 30. 15–21
Ps. 119. 1–8
Eph. 1. 3–10
John 14. 1–14 | *MP*: Ps. 139; 146
Prov. 4. 10–18
James 1. 1–12 | *EP*: Ps. 149
Job 23. 1–12
John 1. 43–end |

2 Tuesday   Athanasius, Bishop of Alexandria, Teacher, 373

| W | Com. Teacher   *or*
also Ecclus. 4. 20–28
Matt. 10. 24–27 | Acts 11. 19–26
Ps. 87
John 10. 22–30 | Ps. 139
alt. **48**; 52
Deut. 9.23 – 10.5
Eph. 4. 17–end | Ps. 115; **116**
alt. Ps. 50
Exod. 32. 15–34
Luke 3. 1–14 |

3 Wednesday

| W | | Acts 12.24 – 13.5
Ps. 67
John 12. 44–end | Ps. 135
alt. Ps. 119. 57–80
Deut. 10. 12–end
Eph. 5. 1–14 | Ps. **47**; 48
alt. Ps. **59**; 60 (67)
Exod. ch. 33
Luke 3. 15–22 |

4 Thursday   English Saints and Martyrs of the Reformation Era

| W | Isa. 43. 1–7   *or*
or Ecclus. 2. 10–17
Ps. 87
2 Cor. 4. 5–12
John 12. 20–26 | Acts 13. 13–25
Ps. 89. 1–2, 20–26
John 13. 16–20 | Ps. 118
alt. 56; **57**; (63†)
Deut. 11. 8–end
Eph. 5. 15–end | Ps. 81; **85**
alt. Ps. 61; **62**; 64
Exod. 34. 1–10, 27–end
Luke 4. 1–13 |

5 Friday

| W | | Acts 13. 26–33
Ps. 2
John 14. 1–6 | Ps. 33
alt. Ps. **51**; 54
Deut. 12. 1–14
Eph. 6. 1–9 | Ps. **36**; 40
alt. Ps. 38
Exod. 35.20 – 36.7
Luke 4. 14–30 |

6 Saturday

| W | | Acts 13. 44–end
Ps. 98. 1–5
John 14. 7–14 | Ps. 34
alt. Ps. 68
Deut. 15. 1–18
Eph. 6. 10–end | Ps. **84**; 86
alt. Ps. 65; **66**
Exod. 40. 17–end
Luke 4. 31–37
ct |

Calendar and Holy Communion	Morning Prayer	Evening Prayer	NOTES
THE THIRD SUNDAY AFTER EASTER			
W Gen. 45. 3–10 Ps. 57 1 Pet. 2. 11–17 John 16. 16–22	Ps. 106. 6–24 Neh. 9. 6–15 1 Cor. 10. 1–13	Ps. 29. 1–10 Ezra 3. 1–13 Eph. 2. 11–end *or First EP of Philip and James* Ps. 119. 1–8 Isa. 40. 27–end John 12. 20–26 **R** ct	
PHILIP AND JAMES, APOSTLES			
R Prov. 4. 10–18 Ps. 25. 1–9 James 1. [1] 2–12 John 14. 1–14	(Ps. 139; 146) Isa. 30. 1–5 John 12. 20–26	(Ps. 149) Job 23. 1–12 John 1. 43–end	
W	Deut. 9.23 – 10.5 Eph. 4. 17–end	Exod. 32. 15–34 Luke 3. 1–14	
The Invention of the Cross			
Wr	Deut. 10. 12–end Eph. 5. 1–14	Exod. ch. 33 Luke 3. 15–22	
W	Deut. 11. 8–end Eph. 5. 15–end	Exod. 34. 1–10, 27–end Luke 4. 1–13	
W	Deut. 12. 1–14 Eph. 6. 1–9	Exod. 35.20 – 36.7 Luke 4. 14–30	
John the Evangelist, ante Portam Latinam CEG of 27 December			
W	Deut. 15. 1–18 Eph. 6. 10–end	Exod. 40. 17–end Luke 4. 31–37	
		ct	

		Sunday Principal Service Weekday Eucharist	Third Service Morning Prayer	Second Service Evening Prayer
7 Sunday	**THE FIFTH SUNDAY OF EASTER**			
W	*The reading from Acts must be used as either the first or second reading at the Principal Service.*	Acts 7. 55–end [or Gen. 8. 1–19] Ps. 31. 1–5, 15–16 (or 31. 1–5) 1 Pet. 2. 2–10 John 14. 1–14	Ps. 30 Ezek. 37. 1–12 John 5. 19–29	Ps. 147. 1–12 Zech. 4. 1–10 Rev. 21. 1–14 *Gospel:* Luke 2. 25–32 [33–38]
8 Monday	**Julian of Norwich, Spiritual Writer, c. 1417**			
W	Com. Religious *or* *also* 1 Cor. 13. 8–end Matt. 5. 13–16	Acts 14. 5–18 Ps. 118. 1–3, 14–15 John 14. 21–26	Ps. 145 *alt.* Ps. 71 Deut. 16. 1–20 1 Pet. 1. 1–12	Ps. 105 *alt.* Ps. **72**; 75 Num. 9. 15–end; 10. 33–end Luke 4. 38–end
9 Tuesday				
W		Acts 14. 19–end Ps. 145. 10–end John 14. 27–end	Ps. *19*; 147. 1–12 *alt.* Ps. 73 Deut. 17. 8–end 1 Pet. 1. 13–end	Ps. 96; **97** *alt.* Ps. 74 Num. 11. 1–33 Luke 5. 1–11
10 Wednesday				
W		Acts 15. 1–6 Ps. 122. 1–5 John 15. 1–8	Ps. *30*; 147. 13–end *alt.* Ps. 77 Deut. 18. 9–end 1 Pet. 2. 1–10	Ps. 98; **99**; 100 *alt.* Ps. 119. 81–104 Num. ch. 12 Luke 5. 12–26
11 Thursday				
W		Acts 15. 7–21 Ps. 96. 1–3, 7–10 John 15. 9–11	Ps. *57*; 148 *alt.* Ps. 78. 1–39† Deut. ch. 19 1 Pet. 2. 11–end	Ps. 104 *alt.* Ps. 78. 40–end† Num. 13. 1–3, 17–end Luke 5. 27–end
12 Friday	*Gregory Dix, Priest, Monk, Scholar, 1952*			
W		Acts 15. 22–31 Ps. 57. 8–end John 15. 12–17	Ps. *138*; 149 *alt.* Ps. 55 Deut. 21.22 – 22.8 1 Pet. 3. 1–12	Ps. 66 *alt.* Ps. 69 Num. 14. 1–25 Luke 6. 1–11
13 Saturday				
W		Acts 16. 1–10 Ps. 100 John 15. 18–21	Ps. *146*; 150 *alt.* Ps. **76**; 79 Deut. 24. 5–end 1 Pet. 3. 13–end	Ps. 118 *alt.* Ps. 81; **84** Num. 14. 26–end Luke 6. 12–26 **ct**
14 Sunday	**THE SIXTH SUNDAY OF EASTER** (Matthias transferred to 15 May)			
W	*The reading from Acts must be used as either the first or second reading at the Principal Service.*	Acts 17. 22–31 [or Gen. 8.20 – 9.17] Ps. 66. 7–end 1 Pet. 3. 13–end John 14. 15–21	Ps. 73. 21–28 Job 14. 1–2, 7–15; 19. 23–27a 1 Thess. 4. 13–end	Ps. 87; 36. 5–10 Zech. 8. 1–13 Rev. 21.22 – 22.5 *Gospel:* John 21. 1–14 *or First EP of Matthias* Ps. 147 Isa. 22. 15–22 Phil. 3.13b – 4.1 **R ct**

Calendar and Holy Communion	Morning Prayer	Evening Prayer	NOTES
THE FOURTH SUNDAY AFTER EASTER			
W Job 19. 21–27a Ps. 66. 14–end James 1. 17–21 John 16. 5–15	Ps. 30 Ezek. 37. 1–12 John 5. 19–29	Ps. 147. 1–12 Zech. 4. 1–10 Rev. 21. 1–14	
W	Deut. 16. 1–20 1 Pet. 1. 1–12	Num. 9. 15–end; 10. 33–end Luke 4. 38–end	
W	Deut. 17. 8–end 1 Pet. 1. 13–end	Num. 11. 1–33 Luke 5. 1–11	
W	Deut. 18. 9–end 1 Pet. 2. 1–10	Num. ch. 12 Luke 5. 12–26	
W	Deut. ch. 19 1 Pet. 2. 11–end	Num. 13. 1–3, 17–end Luke 5. 27–end	
W	Deut. 21.22 – 22.8 1 Pet. 3. 1–12	Num. 14. 1–25 Luke 6. 1–11	
W	Deut. 24. 5–end 1 Pet. 3. 13–end	Num. 14. 26–end Luke 6. 12–26	
		ct	
THE FIFTH SUNDAY AFTER EASTER Rogation Sunday			
W Joel 2. 21–26 Ps. 66. 1–8 James 1. 22–end John 16. 23b–end	Ps. 73. 21–28 Job 14. 1–2, 7–15; 19. 23–27a 1 Thess. 4. 13–end	Ps. 87; 36. 5–10 Zech. 8. 1–13 Rev. 21.22 – 22.5	

	Sunday Principal Service Weekday Eucharist	Third Service Morning Prayer	Second Service Evening Prayer

15 Monday · **MATTHIAS THE APOSTLE** (transferred from 14 May)*
Rogation Day**

R	*The reading from Acts must be used as either the first or second reading at the Eucharist.*	Isa. 22. 15–end or Acts 1. 15–end Ps. 15 Acts 1. 15–end or 1 Cor. 4. 1–7 John 15. 9–17	*MP:* Ps. 16; 147. 1–12 1 Sam. 2. 27–35 Acts 2. 37–end	*EP:* Ps. 80 1 Sam. 16. 1–13a Matt. 7. 15–27
	or, if Matthias is celebrated on 24 February:			
W		Acts 16. 11–15 Ps. 149. 1–5 John 15.26 – 16.4	Ps. *65*; 67 *alt.* Ps. *80*; 82 Deut. ch. 26 1 Pet. 4. 1–11	Ps. *121*; 122; 123 *alt.* Ps. *85*; 86 Num. 16. 1–35 Luke 6. 27–38

16 Tuesday · Rogation Day**
Caroline Chisholm, Social Reformer, 1877

W	Acts 16. 22–34 Ps. 138 John 16. 5–11	Ps. 124; 125; *126*; 127 *alt.* Ps. 87; *89. 1–18* Deut. 28. 1–14 1 Pet. 4. 12–end	Ps. *128*; 129; 130; 131 *alt.* Ps. 89. 19–end Num. 16. 36–end Luke 6. 39–end

17 Wednesday · Rogation Day**

W	Acts 17.15, 22 – 18.1 Ps. 148. 1–2, 11–end John 16. 12–15	Ps. *132*; 133 *alt.* Ps. 119. 105–128 Deut. 28. 58–end 1 Pet. ch. 5	*First EP of Ascension Day* Ps. 15; 24 2 Sam. 23. 1–5 Col. 2.20 – 3.4 𝖂 ct

18 Thursday · **ASCENSION DAY**

𝖂	*The reading from Acts must be used as either the first or second reading at the Eucharist.*	Acts 1. 1–11 or Dan. 7. 9–14 Ps. 47 or Ps. 93 Eph. 1. 15–end or Acts 1. 1–11 Luke 24. 44–end	*MP:* Ps. 110; 150 Isa. 52. 7–end Heb. 7. [11–25] 26–end	*EP:* Ps. 8 Song of the Three 29–37 or 2 Kings 2. 1–15 Rev. ch. 5 *Gospel:* Mark 16. 14–end

19 Friday · Dunstan, Archbishop of Canterbury, Restorer of Monastic Life, 988

W	Com. Bishop *or* *esp.* Matt. 24. 42–46 *also* Exod. 31. 1–5	Acts 18. 9–18 Ps. 47. 1–6 John 16. 20–23	Ps. 20; *81* *alt.* Ps. *88*; (95) Deut. 29. 2–15 1 John 1.1 – 2.6 [Exod. 35.30 – 36.1 Gal. 5. 13–end]***	Ps. 145 *alt.* Ps. 102 Num. 20. 1–13 Luke 7. 11–17

20 Saturday · Alcuin of York, Deacon, Abbot of Tours, 804

W	Com. Religious *or* *also* Col. 3. 12–16 John 4. 19–24	Acts 18. 22–end Ps. 47. 1–2, 7–end John 16. 23–28	Ps. 21; *47* *alt.* Ps. 96; *97*; 100 Deut. ch. 30 1 John 2. 7–17 [Num. 11. 16–17, 24–29 1 Cor. ch. 2]***	Ps. 84; *85* *alt.* Ps. 104 Num. 21. 4–9 Luke 7. 18–35 ct

*Matthias may be celebrated on 24 February instead of 15 May.
**For Rogation Day provision, see p. 11.
***The alternative readings in square brackets may be used at one of the offices, in preparation for the Day of Pentecost.

Calendar and Holy Communion	Morning Prayer	Evening Prayer	NOTES
Rogation Day			
W Job 28. 1–11 Ps. 107. 1–9 James 5. 7–11 Luke 6. 36–42	Deut. ch. 26 1 Pet. 4. 1–11	Num. 16. 1–35 Luke 6. 27–38	
Rogation Day			
W Deut. 8. 1–10 Ps. 121 James 5. 16–end Luke 11. 5–13	Deut. 28. 1–14 1 Pet. 4. 12–end	Num. 16. 36–end Luke 6. 39–end	
Rogation Day			
W Deut. 34. 1–7 Ps. 108. 1–6 Eph. 4. 7–13 John 17. 1–11	Deut. 28. 58–end 1 Pet. ch. 5	*First EP of Ascension Day* Ps. 15; 24 2 Sam. 23. 1–5 Col. 2.20 – 3.4 𝖜 ct	

ASCENSION DAY

𝖜 Dan. 7. 13–14 Ps. 68. 1–6 Acts 1. 1–11 Mark 16. 14–end *or* Luke 24. 44–end	Ps. 110; 150 Isa. 52. 7–end Heb. 7. [11–25] 26–end	Ps. 8 Song of the Three 29–37 *or* 2 Kings 2. 1–15 Rev. ch. 5	
Dunstan, Archbishop of Canterbury, Restorer of Monastic Life, 988			
W Com. Bishop *or* Ascension CEG	Deut. 29. 2–15 1 John 1.1 – 2.6 [Exod. 35.30 – 36.1 Gal. 5. 13–end]***	Num. 20. 1–13 Luke 7. 11–17	
W Ascension CEG	Deut. ch. 30 1 John 2. 7–17 [Num. 11. 16–17, 24–29 1 Cor. ch. 2]*** ct	Num. 21. 4–9 Luke 7. 18–35	

		Sunday Principal Service / Weekday Eucharist	Third Service / Morning Prayer	Second Service / Evening Prayer
21 Sunday	**THE SEVENTH SUNDAY OF EASTER (SUNDAY AFTER ASCENSION DAY)**			
W	*The reading from Acts must be used as either the first or second reading at the Principal Service.*	Acts 1. 6–14 [or Ezek. 36. 24–28] Ps. 68. 1–10, 32–end (or 68. 1–10) 1 Pet. 4. 12–14; 5. 6–11 John 17. 1–11	Ps. 104. 26–35 Isa. 65. 17–end Rev. 21. 1–8	Ps. 47 2 Sam. 23. 1–5 Eph. 1. 15–end *Gospel:* Mark 16. 14–end
22 Monday				
W		Acts 19. 1–8 Ps. 68. 1–6 John 16. 29–end	Ps. *93*; 96; 97 *alt.* Ps. *98*; 99; 101 Deut. 31. 1–13 1 John 2. 18–end [Num. 27. 15–end 1 Cor. ch. 3]*	Ps. 18 *alt.* Ps. *105*† (or 103) Num. 22. 1–35 Luke 7. 36–end
23 Tuesday				
W		Acts 20. 17–27 Ps. 68. 9–10, 18–19 John 17. 1–11	Ps. 98; *99*; 100 *alt.* Ps. *106*† (or 103) Deut. 31. 14–29 1 John 3. 1–10 [1 Sam. 10. 1–10 1 Cor. 12. 1–13]*	Ps. 68 *alt.* Ps. 107† Num. 22.36 – 23.12 Luke 8. 1–15
24 Wednesday	**John and Charles Wesley, Evangelists, Hymn Writers, 1791 and 1788**			
W	Com. Pastor *or* *also* Eph. 5. 15–20	Acts 20. 28–end Ps. 68. 27–28, 32–end John 17. 11–19	Ps. 2; *29* *alt.* Ps. 110; *111*; 112 Deut. 31.30 – 32.14 1 John 3. 11–end [1 Kings 19. 1–18 Matt. 3. 13–end]*	Ps. 36; *46* *alt.* Ps. 119. 129–152 Num. 23. 13–end Luke 8. 16–25
25 Thursday	**The Venerable Bede, Monk at Jarrow, Scholar, Historian, 735** *Aldhelm, Bishop of Sherborne, 709*			
W	Com. Bishop *or* *also* Ecclus. 39. 1–10	Acts 22. 30; 23. 6–11 Ps. 16. 1, 5–end John 17. 20–end	Ps. *24*; 72 *alt.* Ps. 113; *115* Deut. 32. 15–47 1 John 4. 1–6 [Ezek. 11. 14–20 Matt. 9.35 – 10.20]*	Ps. 139 *alt.* Ps. 114; *116*; 117 Num. ch. 24 Luke 8. 26–39
26 Friday	**Augustine, first Archbishop of Canterbury, 605** *John Calvin, Reformer, 1564; Philip Neri, Founder of the Oratorians, Spiritual Guide, 1595*			
W	Com. Religious *or* *also* 1 Thess. 2. 2b–8 Matt. 13. 31–33	Acts 25. 13–21 Ps. 103. 1–2, 11–12, 19–20 John 21. 15–19	Ps. *28*; 30 *alt.* Ps. 139 Deut. ch. 33 1 John 4. 7–end [Ezek. 36. 22–28 Matt. 12. 22–32]*	Ps. 147 *alt.* Ps. *130*; 131; 137 Num. 27. 12–end Luke 8. 40–end
27 Saturday				
W		Acts 28. 16–20, 30–end Ps. 11. 4–end John 21. 20–end	Ps. 42; *43* *alt.* Ps. 120; *121*; 122 Deut. 32. 48–end; ch. 34 1 John ch. 5 [Mic. 3. 1–8 Eph. 6. 10–20]*	*First EP of Pentecost* Ps. 48 Deut. 16. 9–15 John 15.26 – 16.15 **R ct**

*The alternative readings in square brackets may be used at one of the offices, in preparation for the Day of Pentecost.

Calendar and Holy Communion	Morning Prayer	Evening Prayer	NOTES
THE SUNDAY AFTER ASCENSION DAY			
W 2 Kings 2. 9-15 Ps. 68. 32-end 1 Pet. 4. 7-11 John 15.26 - 16.4a	Ps. 104. 26-35 Isa. 65. 17-end Rev. 21. 1-8	Ps. 47 2 Sam. 23. 1-5 Eph. 1. 15-end	
W	Deut. 31. 1-13 1 John 2. 18-end [Num. 27. 15-end 1 Cor. ch. 3]*	Num. 22. 1-35 Luke 7. 36-end	
W	Deut. 31. 14-29 1 John 3. 1-10 [1 Sam. 10. 1-10 1 Cor. 12. 1-13]*	Num. 22.36 - 23.12 Luke 8. 1-15	
W	Deut. 31.30 - 32.14 1 John 3. 11-end [1 Kings 19. 1-18 Matt. 3. 13-end]*	Num. 23. 13-end Luke 8. 16-25	
W	Deut. 32. 15-47 1 John 4. 1-6 [Ezek. 11. 14-20 Matt. 9.35 - 10.20]*	Num. ch. 24 Luke 8. 26-39	
Augustine, first Archbishop of Canterbury, 605			
W Com. Bishop	Deut. ch. 33 1 John 4. 7-end [Ezek. 36. 22-28 Matt. 12. 22-32]*	Num. 27. 12-end Luke 8. 40-end	
The Venerable Bede, Monk at Jarrow, Scholar, Historian, 735			
W Com. Religious	Deut. 32. 48-end; ch. 34 1 John ch. 5 [Mic. 3. 1-8 Eph. 6. 10-20]*	*First EP of Whit Sunday* Ps. 48 Deut. 16. 9-15 John 15.26 - 16.15	
		R ct	

	Sunday Principal Service Weekday Eucharist	Third Service Morning Prayer	Second Service Evening Prayer

28 Sunday   DAY OF PENTECOST (Whit Sunday)

| R | *The reading from Acts must be used as either the first or second reading at the Principal Service.* | Acts 2. 1–21
or Num. 11. 24–30
Ps. 104. 26–36, 37b
(or 104. 26–end)
1 Cor. 12. 3b–13
or Acts 2. 1–21
John 20. 19–23
or John 7. 37–39 | *MP*: Ps. 87
Gen. 11. 1–9
Acts 10. 34–end | *EP*: Ps. 67; 133
Joel 2. 21–end
Acts 2. 14–21 [22–38]
Gospel: Luke 24. 44–end |

29 Monday   Ordinary Time resumes today

| G
DEL 8 | | Ecclus. 17. 24–29
or Jas. 3. 13–end
Ps. 32. 1–8
or Ps. 19. 7–end
Mark 10. 17–27 | Ps. 123; 124; 125; *126*
2 Chron. 17. 1–12
Rom. 1. 1–17 | Ps. *127*; 128; 129
Josh. ch. 1
Luke 9. 18–27 |

30 Tuesday   Josephine Butler, Social Reformer, 1906
Joan of Arc, Visionary, 1431; Apolo Kivebulaya, Evangelist in Central Africa, 1933

| Gw | Com. Saint
esp. Isa. 58. 6–11
also 1 John 3. 18–23
Matt. 9. 10–13 | or Ecclus. 35. 1–12
or Jas. 4. 1–10
Ps. 50. 1–6
or Ps. 55. 7–9, 24
Mark 10. 28–31 | Ps. *132*; 133
2 Chron. 18. 1–27
Rom. 1. 18–end | Ps. (134); *135*
Josh. ch. 2
Luke 9. 28–36
or First EP of The Visit
of Mary to Elizabeth
Ps. 45
Song of Sol. 2. 8–14
Luke 1. 26–38
W ct |

31 Wednesday   THE VISIT OF THE BLESSED VIRGIN MARY TO ELIZABETH*

| W | | Zeph. 3. 14–18
Ps. 113
Rom. 12. 9–16
Luke 1. 39–49 [50–56] | *MP*: Ps. 85; 150
1 Sam. 2. 1–10
Mark 3. 31–end | *EP*: Ps. 122; 127; 128
Zech. 2. 10–end
John 3. 25–30 |
| G | *or, if The Visitation is celebrated on 2, 3 or 4 July:* | Ecclus. 36. 1–2, 4–5,
10–17
or Jas. 4. 13–end
Ps. 79. 8–9, 12, 14
or Ps. 49. 1–2, 5–10
Mark 10. 32–45 | Ps. 119. 153–end
2 Chron. 18.28 - 19.end
Rom. 2. 1–16 | Ps. 136
Josh. ch. 3
Luke 9. 37–50 |

June 2023

1 Thursday   Justin, Martyr at Rome, c. 165

| Gr | Com. Martyr
esp. John 15. 18–21
also 1 Macc. 2. 15–22
1 Cor. 1. 18–25 | or Ecclus. 42. 15–end
or Jas. 5. 1–6
Ps. 33. 1–9
or Ps. 49. 12–20
Mark 10. 46–end | Ps. *143*; 146
2 Chron. 20. 1–23
Rom. 2. 17–end | Ps. *138*; 140; 141
Josh. 4.1 - 5.1
Luke 9. 51–end |

2 Friday

| G | | Ecclus. 44. 1, 9–13
or Jas. 5. 9–12
Ps. 149. 1–5
or Ps. 103. 1–4, 8–13
Mark 11. 11–26 | Ps. *142*; 144
2 Chron. 22.10 - 23.end
Rom. 3. 1–20 | Ps. 145
Josh. 5. 2–end
Luke 10. 1–16 |

*The Visit of the Blessed Virgin Mary to Elizabeth may be celebrated on 2 July or transferred to 4 July or, if Thomas the Apostle is celebrated on 21 December, transferred to 3 July.

May/June 2023

Calendar and Holy Communion	Morning Prayer	Evening Prayer	NOTES
WHIT SUNDAY			
R Deut. 16. 9–12 Ps. 122 Acts 2. 1–11 John 14. 15–31a	Ps. 87 Gen. 11. 1–9 Acts 10. 34–end	Ps. 67; 133 Num. 11. 24–30 Acts 2. 14–21 [22–38]	
Monday in Whitsun Week			
R Acts 10. 34–end John 3. 16–21	Ezek. 11. 14–20 Acts 2. 12–36	Exod. 35.30 – 36.1 Acts 2. 37–end	
Tuesday in Whitsun Week			
R Acts 8. 14–17 John 10. 1–10	Ezek. 37. 1–14 1 Cor. 12. 1–13	2 Sam. 23. 1–5 1 Cor. 12.27 – 13.end	
Ember Day			
R Ember CEG or Acts 2. 14–21 John 6. 44–51	2 Chron. 18.28 – 19.end Rom. 2. 1–16	Josh. ch. 3 Luke 9. 37–50	
Nicomede, Priest and Martyr at Rome (date unknown)			
R Com. Martyr or Acts 2. 22–28 Luke 9. 1–6	2 Chron. 20. 1–23 Rom. 2. 17–end	Josh. 4.1 – 5.1 Luke 9. 51–end	
Ember Day			
R Ember CEG or Acts 8. 5–8 Luke 5. 17–26	2 Chron. 22.10 – 23.end Rom. 3. 1–20	Josh. 5. 2–end Luke 10. 1–16	

		Sunday Principal Service / Weekday Eucharist	Third Service / Morning Prayer	Second Service / Evening Prayer

3 Saturday   *The Martyrs of Uganda, 1885–87 and 1977*

| G | | Ecclus. 51. 12b–20a
or Jas. 5. 13–end
Ps. 19. 7–end
or Ps. 141. 1–4
Mark 11. 27–end | Ps. 147
2 Chron. 24. 1–22
Rom. 3. 21–end | *First EP of Trinity*
Sunday
Ps. 97; 98
Exod. 34. 1–10
Mark 1. 1–13
𝖂 ct |

4 Sunday   **TRINITY SUNDAY**

| 𝖂 | | Isa. 40. 12–17, 27–end
Ps. 8
2 Cor. 13. 11–end
Matt. 28. 16–end | *MP*: Ps. 86. 8–13
Exod. 3. 1–6, 13–15
John 17. 1–11 | *EP*: Ps. 93; 150
Isa. 6. 1–8
John 16. 5–15 |

5 Monday   **Boniface (Wynfrith) of Crediton, Bishop, Apostle of Germany, Martyr, 754**

| Gr
DEL 9 | Com. Martyr   or
also Acts 20. 24–28 | Tob. 1. 1–2; 2. 1–8
or 1 Pet. 1. 3–9
Ps. 15
or Ps. 111
Mark 12. 1–12 | Ps. *1*; 2; 3
2 Chron. 26. 1–21
Rom. 4. 1–12 | Ps. *4*; 7
Josh. 7. 1–15
Luke 10. 25–37 |

6 Tuesday   *Ini Kopuria, Founder of the Melanesian Brotherhood, 1945*

| G | | Tob. 2. 9–end
or 1 Pet. 1. 10–16
Ps. 112
or Ps. 98. 1–5
Mark 12. 13–17 | Ps. *5*; 6; (8)
2 Chron. ch. 28
Rom. 4. 13–end | Ps. *9*; 10†
Josh. 7. 16–end
Luke 10. 38–end |

7 Wednesday

| G | | Tob. 3. 1–11, 16–end
or 1 Pet. 1. 18–25
Ps. 25. 1–8
or Ps. 147. 13–end
Mark 12. 18–27 | Ps. 119. 1–32
2 Chron. 29. 1–19
Rom. 5. 1–11 | Ps. *11*; 12; 13
Josh. 8. 1–29
Luke 11. 1–13
or *First EP of Corpus*
Christi
Ps. 110; 111
Exod. 16. 2–15
John 6. 22–35
W ct |

8 Thursday   **DAY OF THANKSGIVING FOR HOLY COMMUNION (CORPUS CHRISTI)**
Thomas Ken, Bishop of Bath and Wells, Nonjuror, Hymn Writer, 1711

| W – | | Gen. 14. 18–20
Ps. 116. 10–end
1 Cor. 11. 23–26
John 6. 51–58 | *MP*: Ps. 147
Deut. 8. 2–16
1 Cor. 10. 1–17 | *EP*: Ps. 23; 42; 43
Prov. 9. 1–5
Luke 9. 11–17 |
| Gw | *or, if Corpus Christi is not observed:*
Com. Bishop   or
esp. 2 Cor. 4. 1–10
Matt. 24. 42–46 | Tob. 6. 10–11; 7. 1–15;
8. 4–8
or 1 Pet. 2. 2–5, 9–12
Ps. 128
or Ps. 100
Mark 12. 28–34 | Ps. 14; *15*; 16
2 Chron. 29. 20–end
Rom. 5. 12–end | Ps. 18†
Josh. 8. 30–end
Luke 11. 14–28 |

Calendar and Holy Communion	Morning Prayer	Evening Prayer	NOTES
Ember Day			
R Ember CEG or Acts 13. 44–end Matt. 20. 29–end	2 Chron. 24. 1–22 Rom. 3. 21–end	*First EP of Trinity Sunday* Ps. 97; 98 Exod. 34. 1–10 Mark 1. 1–13 𝔚 ct	

TRINITY SUNDAY

𝔚 Isa. 6. 1–8 Ps. 8 Rev. 4. 1–11 John 3. 1–15	Ps. 86. 8–13 Exod. 3. 1–6, 13–15 John 17. 1–11	Ps. 93; 150 Isa. 40. 12–17, 27–end John 16. 5–15	
Boniface (Wynfrith) of Crediton, Bishop, Apostle of Germany, Martyr, 754			
Gr Com. Martyr	2 Chron. 26. 1–21 Rom. 4. 1–12	Josh. 7. 1–15 Luke 10. 25–37	
G	2 Chron. ch. 28 Rom. 4. 13–end	Josh. 7. 16–end Luke 10. 38–end	
G	2 Chron. 29. 1–19 Rom. 5. 1–11	Josh. 8. 1–29 Luke 11. 1–13	
To celebrate Corpus Christi, see *Common Worship* provision.			
G	2 Chron. 29. 20–end Rom. 5. 12–end	Josh. 8. 30–end Luke 11. 14–28	

		Sunday Principal Service Weekday Eucharist	Third Service Morning Prayer	Second Service Evening Prayer
9 Friday		**Columba, Abbot of Iona, Missionary, 597** *Ephrem of Syria, Deacon, Hymn Writer, Teacher, 373*		
	Gw	Com. Missionary *or* Tob. 11. 5–15 *also* Titus 2. 11–end *or* 1 Pet. 4. 7–13 Ps. 146 *or* Ps. 96. 10–end Mark 12. 35–37	Ps. 17; *19* 2 Chron. ch. 30 Rom. 6. 1–14	Ps. 22 Josh. 9. 3–26 Luke 11. 29–36
10 Saturday				
	G	Tob. 12. 1, 5–15, 20a *or* Jude 17, 20–25 Ps. 103. 1, 8–13 *or* Ps. 63. 1–6 Mark 12. 38–end	Ps. 20; 21; *23* 2 Chron. 32. 1–22 Rom. 6. 15–end	Ps. *24*; 25 Josh. 10. 1–15 Luke 11. 37–end **ct** *or First EP of Barnabas* Ps. 1; 15 Isa. 42. 5–12 Acts 14. 8–end **R ct**
11 Sunday		**BARNABAS THE APOSTLE** (or transferred to 12 June)		
	R	Job 29. 11–16 *or* Acts 11. 19–end Ps. 112 Acts 11. 19–end *or* Gal. 2. 1–10 John 15. 12–17	*MP:* Ps. 100; 101; 117 Jer. 9. 23–24 Acts 4. 32–end	*EP:* Ps. 147 Eccles. 12. 9–end *or* Tob. 4. 5–11 Acts 9. 26–31
	G	*or, for The First Sunday after Trinity (Proper 5)* Track 1 Track 2 Gen. 12. 1–9 Hos. 5.15 – 6.6 Ps. 33. 1–12 Ps. 50. 7–15 Rom. 4. 13–end Rom. 4. 13–end Matt. 9. 9–13, 18–26 Matt. 9. 9–13, 18–26	Ps. 38 Deut. 6. 10–25 Acts 22.22 – 23.11	Ps. [39] 41 1 Sam. 18. 1–16 Luke 8. 41–56
12 Monday				
	G **DEL 10**	2 Cor. 1. 1–7 Ps. 34. 1–8 Matt. 5. 1–12	Ps. 27; *30* 2 Chron. 33. 1–13 Rom. 7. 1–6	Ps. 26; *28*; 29 Josh. ch. 14 Luke 12. 1–12
13 Tuesday				
	G	2 Cor. 1. 18–22 Ps. 119. 129–136 Matt. 5. 13–16	Ps. 32; *36* 2 Chron. 34. 1–18 Rom. 7. 7–end	Ps. 33 Josh. 21.43 – 22.8 Luke 12. 13–21
14 Wednesday	*Richard Baxter, Puritan Divine, 1691*			
	G	2 Cor. 3. 4–11 Ps. 78. 1–4 Matt. 5. 17–19	Ps. 34 2 Chron. 34. 19–end Rom. 8. 1–11	Ps. 119. 33–56 Josh. 22. 9–end Luke 12. 22–31
15 Thursday	*Evelyn Underhill, Spiritual Writer, 1941*			
	G	2 Cor. 3.15 – 4.1, 3–6 Ps. 78. 36–40 Matt. 5. 20–26	Ps. 37† 2 Chron. 35. 1–19 Rom. 8. 12–17	Ps. 39; *40* Josh. ch. 23 Luke 12. 32–40
16 Friday		**Richard, Bishop of Chichester, 1253** *Joseph Butler, Bishop of Durham, Philosopher, 1752*		
	Gw	Com. Bishop *or* 2 Cor. 4. 7–15 *also* John 21. 15–19 Ps. 99 Matt. 5. 27–32	Ps. 31 2 Chron. 35.20 – 36.10 Rom. 8. 18–30	Ps. 35 Josh. 24. 1–28 Luke 12. 41–48

Calendar and Holy Communion	Morning Prayer	Evening Prayer	NOTES
G	2 Chron. ch. 30 Rom. 6. 1–14	Josh. 9. 3–26 Luke 11. 29–36	
G	2 Chron. 32. 1–22 Rom. 6. 15–end	Josh. 10. 1–15 Luke 11. 37–end **ct** or First EP of Barnabas Ps. 1; 15 Isa. 42. 5–12 Acts 14. 8–end **R ct**	

BARNABAS THE APOSTLE (or transferred to 12 June)

| R | Job 29. 11–16
Ps. 112
Acts 11. 22–end
John 15. 12–16 | (Ps. 100; 101; 117)
Jer. 9. 23–24
Acts 4. 32–end | (Ps. 147)
Eccles. 12. 9–end
or Tob. 4. 5–11
Acts 9. 26–31 | |

or, for The First Sunday after Trinity

G	2 Sam. 9. 6–end Ps. 41. 1–4 1 John 4. 7–end Luke 16. 19–31	Ps. 38 Deut. 6. 10–25 Acts 22.22 – 23.11	Ps. [39] 41 1 Sam. 18. 1–16 Luke 8. 41–56	
G		2 Chron. 33. 1–13 Rom. 7. 1–6	Josh. ch. 14 Luke 12. 1–12	
G		2 Chron. 34. 1–18 Rom. 7. 7–end	Josh. 21.43 – 22.8 Luke 12. 13–21	
G		2 Chron. 34. 19–end Rom. 8. 1–11	Josh. 22. 9–end Luke 12. 22–31	
G		2 Chron. 35. 1–19 Rom. 8. 12–17	Josh. ch. 23 Luke 12. 32–40	
G		2 Chron. 35.20 – 36.10 Rom. 8. 18–30	Josh. 24. 1–28 Luke 12. 41–48	

	Sunday Principal Service Weekday Eucharist	Third Service Morning Prayer	Second Service Evening Prayer

17 Saturday   *Samuel and Henrietta Barnett, Social Reformers, 1913 and 1936*

| G | 2 Cor. 5. 14–end
Ps. 103. 1–12
Matt. 5. 33–37 | Ps. 41; *42*; 43
2 Chron. 36. 11–end
Rom. 8. 31–end | Ps. 45; *46*
Josh. 24. 29–end
Luke 12. 49–end
ct |

18 Sunday   **THE SECOND SUNDAY AFTER TRINITY (Proper 6)**

| G | *Track 1*
Gen. 18. 1–15 [21. 1–7]
Ps. 116. 1, 10–17 (or
116. 9–17)
Rom. 5. 1–8
Matt. 9.35 – 10.8 [9–23] | *Track 2*
Exod. 19. 2–8a
Ps. 100
Rom. 5. 1–8
Matt. 9.35 – 10.8 [9–23] | Ps. 45
Deut. 10.12 – 11.1
Acts 23. 12–end | Ps. [42]; 43
1 Sam. 21. 1–15
Luke 11. 14–28 |

19 Monday   *Sundar Singh of India, Sadhu (holy man), Evangelist, Teacher, 1929*

| G
DEL 11 | 2 Cor. 6. 1–10
Ps. 98
Matt. 5. 38–42 | Ps. 44
Ezra ch. 1
Rom. 9. 1–18 | Ps. *47*; 49
Judg. ch. 2
Luke 13. 1–9 |

20 Tuesday

| G | 2 Cor. 8. 1–9
Ps. 146
Matt. 5. 43–end | Ps. *48*; 52
Ezra ch. 3
Rom. 9. 19–end | Ps. 50
Judg. 4. 1–23
Luke 13. 10–21 |

21 Wednesday

| G | 2 Cor. 9. 6–11
Ps. 112
Matt. 6. 1–6, 16–18 | Ps. 119. 57–80
Ezra 4. 1–5
Rom. 10. 1–10 | Ps. *59*; 60; (67)
Judg. ch. 5
Luke 13. 22–end |

22 Thursday   **Alban, first Martyr of Britain, c. 250**

| Gr | Com. Martyr   or
esp. 2 Tim. 2. 3–13
John 12. 24–26 | 2 Cor. 11. 1–11
Ps. 111
Matt. 6. 7–15 | Ps. 56; *57*; (63†)
Ezra 4. 7–end
Rom. 10. 11–end | Ps. 61; *62*; 64
Judg. 6. 1–24
Luke 14. 1–11 |

23 Friday   **Etheldreda, Abbess of Ely, c. 678**

| Gw | Com. Religious   or
also Matt. 25. 1–13 | 2 Cor. 11. 18, 21b–30
Ps. 34. 1–6
Matt. 6. 19–23 | Ps. *51*; 54
Ezra ch. 5
Rom. 11. 1–12 | Ps. 38
Judg. 6. 25–end
Luke 14. 12–24
*or First EP of The Birth
of John the Baptist*
Ps. 71
Judg. 13. 2–7, 24–end
Luke 1. 5–25
W ct |

24 Saturday   **THE BIRTH OF JOHN THE BAPTIST**

| W | Isa. 40. 1–11
Ps. 85. 7–end
Acts 13. 14b–26
or Gal. 3. 23–end
Luke 1. 57–66, 80 | *MP*: Ps. 50; 149
Ecclus. 48. 1–10
or Mal. 3. 1–6
Luke 3. 1–17 | *EP*: Ps. 80; 82
Mal. ch. 4
Matt. 11. 2–19 |

25 Sunday   **THE THIRD SUNDAY AFTER TRINITY (Proper 7)**

| G | *Track 1*
Gen. 21. 8–21
Ps. 86. 1–10, 16–end
(or 86. 1–10)
Rom. 6. 1b–11
Matt. 10. 24–39 | *Track 2*
Jer. 20. 7–13
Ps. 69. 8–11 [12–17]
18–20 (or 69. 14–20)
Rom. 6. 1b–11
Matt. 10. 24–39 | Ps. 49
Deut. 11. 1–15
Acts 27. 1–12 | Ps. 46; [48]
1 Sam. 24. 1–17
Luke 14. 12–24 |

	Calendar and Holy Communion	Morning Prayer	Evening Prayer	NOTES
	Alban, first Martyr of Britain, c. 250			
Gr	Com. Martyr	2 Chron. 36. 11–end Rom. 8. 31–end	Josh. 24. 29–end Luke 12. 49–end	
			ct	
	THE SECOND SUNDAY AFTER TRINITY			
G	Gen. 12. 1–4 Ps. 120 1 John 3. 13–end Luke 14. 16–24	Ps. 45 Deut. 10.12 – 11.1 Acts 23. 12–end	Ps. [42]; 43 1 Sam. 21. 1–15 Luke 11. 14–28	
G		Ezra ch. 1 Rom. 9. 1–18	Judg. ch. 2 Luke 13. 1–9	
	Translation of Edward, King of the West Saxons, 979			
Gr	Com. Martyr	Ezra ch. 3 Rom. 9. 19–end	Judg. 4. 1–23 Luke 13. 10–21	
G		Ezra 4. 1–5 Rom. 10. 1–10	Judg. ch. 5 Luke 13. 22–end	
G		Ezra 4. 7–end Rom. 10. 11–end	Judg. 6. 1–24 Luke 14. 1–11	
G		Ezra ch. 5 Rom. 11. 1–12	Judg. 6. 25–end Luke 14. 12–24 or First EP of The Nativity of John the Baptist (Ps. 71) Judg. 13. 2–7, 24–end Luke 1. 5–25 **W ct**	
	THE NATIVITY OF JOHN THE BAPTIST			
W	Isa. 40. 1–11 Ps. 80. 1–7 Acts 13. 22–26 Luke 1. 57–80	(Ps. 50; 149) Ecclus. 48. 1–10 or Mal. 3. 1–6 Luke 3. 1–17	(Ps. 82) Mal. ch. 4 Matt. 11. 2–19	
	THE THIRD SUNDAY AFTER TRINITY			
G	2 Chron. 33. 9–13 Ps. 55. 17–23 1 Pet. 5. 5b–11 Luke 15. 1–10	Ps. 49 Deut. 11. 1–15 Acts 27. 1–12	Ps. 46; [48] 1 Sam. 24. 1–17 Luke 14. 1–14	

		Sunday Principal Service Weekday Eucharist	Third Service Morning Prayer	Second Service Evening Prayer
26 Monday				
G **DEL 12**		Gen. 12. 1–9 Ps. 33. 12–end Matt. 7. 1–5	Ps. 71 Ezra ch. 7 Rom. 11. 25–end	Ps. **72**; 75 Judg. 8. 22–end Luke 15. 1–10
27 Tuesday	*Cyril, Bishop of Alexandria, Teacher, 444*			
G		Gen. 13. 2, 5–end Ps. 15 Matt. 7. 6, 12–14	Ps. 73 Ezra 8. 15–end Rom. 12. 1–8	Ps. 74 Judg. 9. 1–21 Luke 15. 11–end
28 Wednesday	Irenaeus, Bishop of Lyons, Teacher, c. 200 Ember Day*			
Gw *or* **Rw**	Com. Teacher *or* *also* 2 Pet. 1. 16–end	Gen. 15. 1–12, 17–18 Ps. 105. 1–9 Matt. 7. 15–20	Ps. 77 Ezra ch. 9 Rom. 12. 9–end	Ps. 119. 81–104 Judg. 9. 22–end Luke 16. 1–18 *or First EP of Peter and Paul* Ps. 66; 67 Ezek. 3. 4–11 Gal. 1.13 – 2.8 *or, for Peter alone:* Acts 9. 32–end **R ct**
29 Thursday	**PETER AND PAUL, APOSTLES**			
R		Zech. 4. 1–6a, 10b–end *or* Acts 12. 1–11 Ps. 125 Acts 12. 1–11 *or* 2 Tim. 4. 6–8, 17–18 Matt. 16. 13–19	*MP*: Ps. 71; 113 Isa. 49. 1–6 Acts 11. 1–18	*EP*: Ps. 124; 138 Ezek. 34. 11–16 John 21. 15–22
R	*or, if Peter is commemorated alone:*	Ezek. 3. 22–end *or* Acts 12. 1–11 Ps. 125 Acts 12. 1–11 *or* 1 Pet. 2. 19–end Matt. 16. 13–19	*MP*: Ps. 71; 113 Isa. 49. 1–6 Acts 11. 1–18	*EP*: Ps. 124; 138 Ezek. 34. 11–16 John 21. 15–22
30 Friday	Ember Day*			
G *or* **R**		Gen. 17. 1, 9–10, 15–22 Ps. 128 Matt. 8. 1–4	Ps. 55 Neh. ch. 1 Rom. 13. 8–end	Ps. 69 Judg. 11. 29–end Luke 17. 1–10

July 2023

		Sunday Principal Service Weekday Eucharist	Third Service Morning Prayer	Second Service Evening Prayer
1 Saturday	Ember Day* Henry, John and Henry Venn the Younger, Priests, Evangelical Divines, 1797, 1813 and 1873			
G *or* **R**		Gen. 18. 1–15 *Canticle*: Luke 1. 46b–55 Matt. 8. 5–17	Ps. **76**; 79 Neh. ch. 2 Rom. 14. 1–12	Ps. 81; **84** Judg. 12. 1–7 Luke 17. 11–19 **ct**

*For Ember Day provision, see p. 11.

Calendar and Holy Communion	Morning Prayer	Evening Prayer	NOTES
G	Ezra ch. 7 Rom. 11. 25–end	Judg. 8. 22–end Luke 15. 1–10	
G	Ezra 8. 15–end Rom. 12. 1–8	Judg. 9. 1–21 Luke 15. 11–end	
G	Ezra ch. 9 Rom. 12. 9–end	Judg. 9. 22–end Luke 16. 1–18 *or First EP of Peter* (Ps. 66; 67) Ezek. 3. 4–11 Acts 9. 32–end	
		R ct	
PETER THE APOSTLE			
R Ezek. 3. 4–11 Ps. 125 Acts 12. 1–11 Matt. 16. 13–19	(Ps. 71; 113) Isa. 49. 1–6 Acts 11. 1–18	(Ps. 124; 138) Ezek. 34. 11–16 John 21. 15–22	
G	Neh. ch. 1 Rom. 13. 8–end	Judg. 11. 29–end Luke 17. 1–10	
G	Neh. ch. 2 Rom. 14. 1–12	Judg. 12. 1–7 Luke 17. 11–19	
		ct	

		Sunday Principal Service / Weekday Eucharist	Third Service / Morning Prayer	Second Service / Evening Prayer

2 Sunday — THE FOURTH SUNDAY AFTER TRINITY (Proper 8)*

G	*Track 1*	*Track 2*	Ps. 52; 53	Ps. 50 (*or* 50. 1–15)
	Gen. 22. 1–14	Jer. 28. 5–9	Deut. 15. 1–11	1 Sam. 28. 3–19
	Ps. 13	Ps. 89. 1–4, 15–18	Acts 27. [13–32] 33–end	Luke 17. 20–end
	Rom. 6. 12–end	(*or* 89. 8–18)		*or First EP of Thomas*
	Matt. 10. 40–end	Rom. 6. 12–end		Ps. 27
		Matt. 10. 40–end		Isa. ch. 35
				Heb. 10.35 – 11.1
				R ct

3 Monday — THOMAS THE APOSTLE**

R		Hab. 2. 1–4	*MP*: Ps. 92; 146	*EP*: Ps. 139
DEL 13		Ps. 31. 1–6	2 Sam. 15. 17–21	Job 42. 1–6
		Eph. 2. 19–end	*or* Ecclus. ch. 2	1 Pet. 1. 3–12
		John 20. 24–29	John 11. 1–16	
		or, if Thomas is not celebrated:		
G		Gen. 18. 16–end	Ps. **80**; 82	Ps. **85**; 86
		Ps. 103. 6–17	Neh. ch. 4	Judg. 13. 1–24
		Matt. 8. 18–22	Rom. 14. 13–end	Luke 17. 20–end

4 Tuesday

G	Gen. 19. 15–29	Ps. 87; **89. 1–18**	Ps. 89. 19–end
	Ps. 26	Neh. ch. 5	Judg. ch. 14
	Matt. 8. 23–27	Rom. 15. 1–13	Luke 18. 1–14

5 Wednesday

G	Gen. 21. 5, 8–20	Ps. 119. 105–128	Ps. **91**; 93
	Ps. 34. 1–12	Neh. 6.1 – 7.4	Judg. 15.1 – 16.3
	Matt. 8. 28–end	Rom. 15. 14–21	Luke 18. 15–30

6 Thursday — *Thomas More, Scholar, and John Fisher, Bishop of Rochester, Reformation Martyrs, 1535*

G	Gen. 22. 1–19	Ps. 90; **92**	Ps. 94
	Ps. 116. 1–7	Neh. 7.73b – 8.end	Judg. 16. 4–end
	Matt. 9. 1–8	Rom. 15. 22–end	Luke 18. 31–end

7 Friday — ***

G	Gen. 23. 1–4, 19;	Ps. **88**; (95)	Ps. 102
	24. 1–8, 62–end	Neh. 9. 1–23	Judg. ch. 17
	Ps. 106. 1–5	Rom. 16. 1–16	Luke 19. 1–10
	Matt. 9. 9–13		

8 Saturday

G	Gen. 27. 1–5a, 15–29	Ps. 96; **97**; 100	Ps. 104
	Ps. 135. 1–6	Neh. 9. 24–end	Judg. 18. 1–20, 27–end
	Matt. 9. 14–17	Rom. 16. 17–end	Luke 19. 11–27
			ct

9 Sunday — THE FIFTH SUNDAY AFTER TRINITY (Proper 9)

G	*Track 1*	*Track 2*	Ps. 55. 1–15, 18–22	Ps. 56; [57]
	Gen. 24. 34–38,	Zech. 9. 9–12	Deut. 24. 10–end	2 Sam. 2. 1–11; 3. 1
	42–49, 58–end	Ps. 145. 8–15	Acts 28. 1–16	Luke 18.31 – 19.10
	Ps. 45. 10–end	Rom. 7. 15–25a		
	or Canticle: Song of	Matt. 11. 16–19, 25–30		
	Sol. 2. 8–13			
	Rom. 7. 15–25a			
	Matt. 11. 16–19, 25–end			

*The Visit of the Blessed Virgin Mary to Elizabeth may be celebrated on 2 July or transferred to 3 July (if Thomas the Apostle is celebrated on 21 December) or 4 July instead of 31 May.
**Thomas the Apostle may be celebrated on 21 December instead of 3 July.
***Thomas Becket may be celebrated on 7 July instead of 29 December.

Calendar and Holy Communion	Morning Prayer	Evening Prayer

THE FOURTH SUNDAY AFTER TRINITY

G Gen. 3. 17-19 Ps. 79. 8-10 Rom. 8. 18-23 Luke 6. 36-42	Ps. 52; 53 Deut. 15. 1-11 Acts 27. [13-32] 33-end	Ps. 50 (or 50. 1-15) 1 Sam. 28. 3-19 Luke 17. 20-end
G	Neh. ch. 4 Rom. 14. 13-end	Judg. 13. 1-24 Luke 17. 20-end

Translation of Martin, Bishop of Tours, c. 397

Gw Com. Bishop	Neh. ch. 5 Rom. 15. 1-13	Judg. ch. 14 Luke 18. 1-14
G	Neh. 6.1 - 7.4 Rom. 15. 14-21	Judg. 15.1 - 16.3 Luke 18. 15-30
G	Neh. 7.73b - 8.end Rom. 15. 22-end	Judg. 16. 4-end Luke 18. 31-end
G	Neh. 9. 1-23 Rom. 16. 1-16	Judg. ch. 17 Luke 19. 1-10
G	Neh. 9. 24-end Rom. 16. 17-end	Judg. 18. 1-20, 27-end Luke 19. 11-27
		ct

THE FIFTH SUNDAY AFTER TRINITY

G 1 Kings 19. 19-21 Ps. 84. 8-end 1 Pet. 3. 8-15a Luke 5. 1-11	Ps. 55. 1-15, 18-22 Deut. 24. 10-end Acts 28. 1-16	Ps. 56; [57] 2 Sam. 2. 1-11; 3. 1 Luke 18.31 - 19.10

	Sunday Principal Service Weekday Eucharist	Third Service Morning Prayer	Second Service Evening Prayer
10 Monday			
G **DEL 14**	Gen. 28. 10–end Ps. 91. 1–10 Matt. 9. 18–26	Ps. *98*; 99; 101 Neh. 12. 27–47 2 Cor. 1. 1–14	Ps. 105† (*or* 103) 1 Sam. 1. 1–20 Luke 19. 28–40
11 Tuesday	**Benedict of Nursia, Abbot of Monte Cassino, Father of Western Monasticism, c. 550**		
Gw	Com. Religious *or* *also* 1 Cor. 3. 10–11 Luke 18. 18–22	Gen. 32. 22–end Ps. 17. 1–8 Matt. 9. 32–end	Ps. *106*†; (*or* 103) Neh. 13. 1–14 2 Cor. 1.15 – 2.4	Ps. 107† 1 Sam. 1.21 – 2.11 Luke 19. 41–end
12 Wednesday			
G	Gen. 41. 55–end; 42. 5–7, 17–end Ps. 33. 1–4, 18–end Matt. 10. 1–7	Ps. 110; *111*; 112 Neh. 13. 15–end 2 Cor. 2. 5–end	Ps. 119. 129–152 1 Sam. 2. 12–26 Luke 20. 1–8
13 Thursday			
G	Gen. 44. 18–21, 23–29; 45. 1–5 Ps. 105. 11–17 Matt. 10. 7–15	Ps. 113; *115* Esth. ch. 1 2 Cor. ch. 3	Ps. 114; *116*; 117 1 Sam. 2. 27–end Luke 20. 9–19
14 Friday	**John Keble, Priest, Tractarian, Poet, 1866**		
Gw	Com. Pastor *or* *also* Lam. 3. 19–26 Matt. 5. 1–8	Gen. 46. 1–7, 28–30 Ps. 37. 3–6, 27–28 Matt. 10. 16–23	Ps. 139 Esth. ch. 2 2 Cor. ch. 4	Ps. *130*; 131; 137 1 Sam. 3.1 – 4.1a Luke 20. 20–26
15 Saturday	**Swithun, Bishop of Winchester, c. 862** *Bonaventure, Friar, Bishop, Teacher, 1274*		
Gw	Com. Bishop *or* *also* James 5. 7–11, 13–18	Gen. 49. 29–end; 50. 15–25 Ps. 105. 1–7 Matt. 10. 24–33	Ps. 120; *121*; 122 Esth. ch. 3 2 Cor. ch. 5	Ps. 118 1 Sam. 4. 1b–end Luke 20. 27–40 **ct**
16 Sunday	**THE SIXTH SUNDAY AFTER TRINITY (Proper 10)**		
G	*Track 1* Gen. 25. 19–end Ps. 119. 105–112 Rom. 8. 1–11 Matt. 13. 1–9, 18–23	*Track 2* Isa. 55. 10–13 Ps. 65 (*or* 65. 8–end) Rom. 8. 1–11 Matt. 13. 1–9, 18–23	Ps. 64; 65 Deut. 28. 1–14 Acts 28. 17–end	Ps. 60; [63] 2 Sam. 7. 18–end Luke 19.41 – 20.8
17 Monday			
G **DEL 15**	Exod. 1. 8–14, 22 Ps. 124 Matt. 10.34 – 11.1	Ps. 123; 124; 125; *126* Esth. ch. 4 2 Cor. 6.1 – 7.1	Ps. *127*; 128; 129 1 Sam. ch. 5 Luke 20.41 – 21.4
18 Tuesday	*Elizabeth Ferard, first Deaconess of the Church of England, Founder of the Community of St Andrew, 1883*		
G	Exod. 2. 1–15 Ps. 69. 1–2, 31–end Matt. 11. 20–24	Ps. *132*; 133 Esth. ch. 5 2 Cor. 7. 2–end	Ps. (134); *135* 1 Sam. 6. 1–16 Luke 21. 5–19
19 Wednesday	**Gregory, Bishop of Nyssa, and his sister Macrina, Deaconess, Teachers, c. 394 and c. 379**		
Gw	Com. Teacher *or* *esp.* 1 Cor. 2. 9–13 *also* Wisd. 9. 13–17	Exod. 3. 1–6, 9–12 Ps. 103. 1–7 Matt. 11. 25–27	Ps. 119. 153–end Esth. 6. 1–13 2 Cor. 8. 1–15	Ps. 136 1 Sam. ch. 7 Luke 21. 20–28

Calendar and Holy Communion	Morning Prayer	Evening Prayer	NOTES
G	Neh. 12. 27–47 2 Cor. 1. 1–14	1 Sam. 1. 1–20 Luke 19. 28–40	
G	Neh. 13. 1–14 2 Cor. 1.15 – 2.4	1 Sam. 1.21 – 2.11 Luke 19. 41–end	
G	Neh. 13. 15–end 2 Cor. 2. 5–end	1 Sam. 2. 12–26 Luke 20. 1–8	
G	Esth. ch. 1 2 Cor. ch. 3	1 Sam. 2. 27–end Luke 20. 9–19	
G	Esth. ch. 2 2 Cor. ch. 4	1 Sam. 3.1 – 4.1a Luke 20. 20–26	
Swithun, Bishop of Winchester, c. 862			
Gw Com. Bishop	Esth. ch. 3 2 Cor. ch. 5	1 Sam. 4. 1b–end Luke 20. 27–40	
		ct	
THE SIXTH SUNDAY AFTER TRINITY			
G Gen. 4. 2b–15 Ps. 90. 12–end Rom. 6. 3–11 Matt. 5. 20–26	Ps. 64; 65 Deut. 28. 1–14 Acts 28. 17–end	Ps. 60; [63] 2 Sam. 7. 18–end Luke 20. 1–8	
G	Esth. ch. 4 2 Cor. 6.1 – 7.1	1 Sam. ch. 5 Luke 20.41 – 21.4	
G	Esth. ch. 5 2 Cor. 7. 2–end	1 Sam. 6. 1–16 Luke 21. 5–19	
G	Esth. 6. 1–13 2 Cor. 8. 1–15	1 Sam. ch. 7 Luke 21. 20–28	

		Sunday Principal Service / Weekday Eucharist	Third Service / Morning Prayer	Second Service / Evening Prayer

20 Thursday   *Margaret of Antioch, Martyr, 4th century; Bartolomé de las Casas, Apostle to the Indies, 1566*

| G | | Exod. 3. 13–20
Ps. 105. 1, 5, 8–9, 24–27
Matt. 11. 28–end | Ps. *143*; 146
Esth. 6.14 – 7.end
2 Cor. 8.16 – 9.5 | Ps. *138*; 140; 141
1 Sam. ch. 8
Luke 21. 29–end |

21 Friday

| G | | Exod. 11.10 – 12.14
Ps. 116. 10–end
Matt. 12. 1–8 | Ps. 142; *144*
Esth. ch. 8
2 Cor. 9. 6–end | Ps. 145
1 Sam. 9. 1–14
Luke 22. 1–13
or *First EP of Mary Magdalene*
Ps. 139
Isa. 25. 1–9
2 Cor. 1. 3–7
W ct |

22 Saturday   **MARY MAGDALENE**

| W | | Song of Sol. 3. 1–4
Ps. 42. 1–10
2 Cor. 5. 14–17
John 20. 1–2, 11–18 | *MP*: Ps. 30; 32; 150
1 Sam. 16. 14–end
Luke 8. 1–3 | *EP*: Ps. 63
Zeph. 3. 14–end
Mark 15.40 – 16.7 |

23 Sunday   **THE SEVENTH SUNDAY AFTER TRINITY (Proper 11)**

| G | | *Track 1*
Gen. 28. 10–19a
Ps. 139. 1–11, 23–24
(or 139. 1–11)
Rom. 8. 12–25
Matt. 13. 24–30, 36–43 | *Track 2*
Wisd. 12. 13, 16–19
or Isa. 44. 6–8
Ps. 86. 11–end
Rom. 8. 12–25
Matt. 13. 24–30, 36–43 | Ps. 71
Deut. 30. 1–10
1 Pet. 3. 8–18 | Ps. 67; [70]
1 Kings 2. 10–12;
3. 16–end
Acts 4. 1–22
Gospel: Mark 6. 30–34, 53–end |

24 Monday

| G
DEL 16 | | Exod. 14. 5–18
Ps. 136. 1–4, 10–15
or *Canticle*: Exod. 15. 1–6
Matt. 12. 38–42 | Ps. *1*; 2; 3
Jer. ch. 26
2 Cor. 11. 1–15 | Ps. *4*; 7
1 Sam. 10. 1–16
Luke 22. 24–30
or *First EP of James*
Ps. 144
Deut. 30. 11–end
Mark 5. 21–end
R ct |

25 Tuesday   **JAMES THE APOSTLE**

| R | | Jer. 45. 1–5
or Acts 11.27 – 12.2
Ps. 126
Acts 11.27 – 12.2
or 2 Cor. 4. 7–15
Matt. 20. 20–28 | *MP*: Ps. 7; 29; 117
2 Kings 1. 9–15
Luke 9. 46–56 | *EP*: Ps. 94
Jer. 26. 1–15
Mark 1. 14–20 |

26 Wednesday   **Anne and Joachim, Parents of the Blessed Virgin Mary**

| Gw | | Zeph. 3. 14–18a   or
Ps. 127
Rom. 8. 28–30
Matt. 13. 16–17 | Exod. 16. 1–5, 9–15
Ps. 78. 17–31
Matt. 13. 1–9 | Ps. 119. 1–32
Jer. 29. 1–14
2 Cor. ch. 12 | Ps. *11*; 12; 13
1 Sam. ch. 11
Luke 22. 39–46 |

27 Thursday   *Brooke Foss Westcott, Bishop of Durham, Teacher, 1901*

| G | | Exod. 19. 1–2, 9–11, 16–20
Canticle: Bless the Lord
Matt. 13. 10–17 | Ps. 14; *15*; 16
Jer. 30. 1–11
2 Cor. ch. 13 | Ps. 18†
1 Sam. ch. 12
Luke 22. 47–62 |

Calendar and Holy Communion	Morning Prayer	Evening Prayer
Margaret of Antioch, Martyr, 4th century		
Gr Com. Virgin Martyr	Esth. 6.14 – 7.end	1 Sam. ch. 8
	2 Cor. 8.16 – 9.5	Luke 21. 29–end
G	Esth. ch. 8	1 Sam. 9. 1–14
	2 Cor. 9. 6–end	Luke 22. 1–13
		or First EP of Mary Magdalene
		(Ps. 139)
		Isa. 25. 1–9
		2 Cor. 1. 3–7
		W ct
MARY MAGDALENE		
W Zeph. 3. 14–end	(Ps. 30; 32; 150)	(Ps. 63)
Ps. 30. 1–5	1 Sam. 16. 14–end	Song of Sol. 3. 1–4
2 Cor. 5. 14–17	Luke 8. 1–3	Mark 15.40 – 16.7
John 20. 11–18		
THE SEVENTH SUNDAY AFTER TRINITY		
G 1 Kings 17. 8–16	Ps. 71	Ps. 67; [70]
Ps. 34. 11–end	Deut. 30. 1–10	1 Kings 2. 10–12;
Rom. 6. 19–end	1 Pet. 3. 13–22	3. 16–end
Mark 8. 1–10a		Acts 4. 1–22
G	Jer. ch. 26	1 Sam. 10. 1–16
	2 Cor. 11. 1–15	Luke 22. 24–30
		or First EP of James
		(Ps. 144)
		Deut. 30. 11–end
		Mark 5. 21–end
		R ct
JAMES THE APOSTLE		
R 2 Kings 1. 9–15	(Ps. 7; 29; 117)	(Ps. 94)
Ps. 15	Jer. 45. 1–5	Jer. 26. 1–15
Acts 11.27 – 12.3a	Luke 9. 46–56	Mark 1. 14–20
Matt. 20. 20–28		
Anne, Mother of the Blessed Virgin Mary		
Gw Com. Saint	Jer. 29. 1–14	1 Sam. ch. 11
	2 Cor. ch. 12	Luke 22. 39–46
G	Jer. 30. 1–11	1 Sam. ch. 12
	2 Cor. ch. 13	Luke 22. 47–62

NOTES

		Sunday Principal Service Weekday Eucharist	Third Service Morning Prayer	Second Service Evening Prayer
28 Friday				
G		Exod. 20. 1–17 Ps. 19. 7–11 Matt. 13. 18–23	Ps. 17; *19* Jer. 30. 12–22 James 1. 1–11	Ps. 22 1 Sam. 13. 5–18 Luke 22. 63–end
29 Saturday	Mary, Martha and Lazarus, Companions of our Lord			
Gw	Isa. 25. 6–9 *or* Ps. 49. 5–10, 16 Heb. 2. 10–15 John 12. 1–8	Exod. 24. 3–8 Ps. 50. 1–6, 14–15 Matt. 13. 24–30	Ps. 20; 21; *23* Jer. 31. 1–22 James 1. 12–end	Ps. *24*; 25 1 Sam. 13.19 – 14.15 Luke 23. 1–12 ct
30 Sunday	**THE EIGHTH SUNDAY AFTER TRINITY (Proper 12)**			
G	*Track 1* Gen. 29. 15–28 Ps. 105. 1–11, 45b (or 105. 1–11) or Ps. 128 Rom. 8. 26–end Matt. 13. 31–33, 44–52	*Track 2* 1 Kings 3. 5–12 Ps. 119. 129–136 Rom. 8. 26–39 Matt. 13. 31–33, 44–52	Ps. 77 Song of Sol. ch. 2 or 1 Macc. 2. [1–14] 15–22 1 Pet. 4. 7–14	Ps. 75; [76] 1 Kings 6. 11–14, 23–end Acts 12. 1–17 *Gospel:* John 6. 1–21
31 Monday	Ignatius of Loyola, Founder of the Society of Jesus, 1556			
G **DEL 17**		Exod. 32. 15–24, 30–34 Ps. 106. 19–23 Matt. 13. 31–35	Ps. 27; *30* Jer. 31. 23–25, 27–37 James 2. 1–13	Ps. 26; *28*; 29 1 Sam. 14. 24–46 Luke 23. 13–25

August 2023

1 Tuesday				
G		Exod. 33. 7–11; 34. 5–9, 28 Ps. 103. 8–12 Matt. 13. 36–43	Ps. 32; *36* Jer. 32. 1–15 James 2. 14–end	Ps. 33 1 Sam. 15. 1–23 Luke 23. 26–43
2 Wednesday				
G		Exod. 34. 29–end Ps. 99 Matt. 13. 44–46	Ps. 34 Jer. 33. 1–13 James ch. 3	Ps. 119. 33–56 1 Sam. ch. 16 Luke 23. 44–56a
3 Thursday				
G		Exod. 40. 16–21, 34–end Ps. 84. 1–6 Matt. 13	Ps. 37† Jer. 33. 14–end James 4. 1–12	Ps. 39; *40* 1 Sam. 17. 1–30 Luke 23.56b – 24.12
4 Friday	John-Baptiste Vianney, Curé d'Ars, Spiritual Guide, 1859			
G		Lev. 23. 1, 4–11, 15–16, 27, 34–37 Ps. 81. 1–8 Matt. 13. 54–end	Ps. 31 Jer. ch. 35 James 4.13 – 5.6	Ps. 35 1 Sam. 17. 31–54 Luke 24. 13–35
5 Saturday	Oswald, King of Northumbria, Martyr, 642			
Gr	Com. Martyr *or* *esp.* 1 Pet. 4. 12–end John 16. 29–end	Lev. 25. 1, 8–17 Ps. 67 Matt. 14. 1–12	Ps. 41; *42*; 43 Jer. 36. 1–18 James 5. 7–end	Ps. 45; *46* 1 Sam. 17.55 – 18.16 Luke 24. 36–end ct *or First EP of The Transfiguration* Ps. 99; 110 Exod. 24. 12–end John 12. 27–36a 𝔚 ct

Calendar and Holy Communion	Morning Prayer	Evening Prayer	NOTES
G	Jer. 30. 12–22 James 1. 1–11	1 Sam. 13. 5–18 Luke 22. 63–end	
G	Jer. 31. 1–22 James 1. 12–end	1 Sam. 13.19 – 14.15 Luke 23. 1–12 ct	

THE EIGHTH SUNDAY AFTER TRINITY

Calendar and Holy Communion	Morning Prayer	Evening Prayer	NOTES
G Jer. 23. 16–24 Ps. 31. 1–6 Rom. 8. 12–17 Matt. 7. 15–21	Ps. 77 Song of Sol. ch. 2 or 1 Macc. 2. [1–14] 15–22 1 Pet. 4. 7–14	Ps. 75; [76] 1 Kings 6. 11–14, 23–end Acts 12. 1–17	
G	Jer. 31. 23–25, 27–37 James 2. 1–13	1 Sam. 14. 24–46 Luke 23. 13–25	
Lammas Day			
G	Jer. 32. 1–15 James 2. 14–end	1 Sam. 15. 1–23 Luke 23. 26–43	
G	Jer. 33. 1–13 James ch. 3	1 Sam. ch. 16 Luke 23. 44–56a	
G	Jer. 33. 14–end James 4. 1–12	1 Sam. 17. 1–30 Luke 23.56b – 24.12	
G	Jer. ch. 35 James 4.13 – 5.6	1 Sam. 17. 31–54 Luke 24. 13–35	
G	Jer. 36. 1–18 James 5. 7–end	1 Sam. 17.55 – 18.16 Luke 24. 36–end ct *or First EP of The Transfiguration* (Ps. 99; 110) Exod. 24. 12–end John 12. 27–36a 𝔚 ct	

		Sunday Principal Service Weekday Eucharist	Third Service Morning Prayer	Second Service Evening Prayer
6 Sunday	**THE TRANSFIGURATION OF OUR LORD** (or transferred to 7 August)			
w		Dan. 7. 9–10, 13–14 Ps. 97 2 Pet. 1. 16–19 Luke 9. 28–36	*MP*: Ps. 27; 150 Ecclus. 48. 1–10 *or* 1 Kings 19. 1–16 1 John 3. 1–3	*EP*: Ps. 72 Exod. 34. 29–end 2 Cor. ch. 3
G	*or, for The Ninth Sunday after Trinity (Proper 13):* *Track 1* Gen. 32. 22–31 Ps. 17. 1–7, 16 (or 17. 1–7) Rom. 9. 1–5 Matt. 14. 13–21	*Track 2* Isa. 55. 1–5 Ps. 145. 8–9, 15–end (or 145. 15–end) Rom. 9. 1–5 Matt. 14. 13–21	Ps. 85 Song of Sol. 5. 2–end *or* 1 Macc. 3. 1–12 2 Pet. 1. 1–15	Ps. 80 (or 80. 1–8) 1 Kings 10. 1–13 Acts 13. 1–13 *Gospel*: John 6. 24–35
7 Monday	For The Transfiguration of Our Lord, see 6 August. *John Mason Neale, Priest, Hymn Writer, 1866*			
G **DEL 18**		Num. 11. 4–15 Ps. 81. 11–end Matt. 14. 13–21 *or* Matt. 14. 22–end	Ps. 44 Jer. 36. 19–end Mark 1. 1–13	Ps. *47*; 49 1 Sam. 19. 1–18 Acts 1. 1–14
8 Tuesday	**Dominic, Priest, Founder of the Order of Preachers, 1221**			
Gw	Com. Religious *or* *also* Ecclus. 39. 1–10	Num. 12. 1–13 Ps. 51. 1–8 Matt. 14. 22–end *or* Matt. 15. 1–2, 10–14	Ps. *48*; 52 Jer. ch. 37 Mark 1. 14–20	Ps. 50 1 Sam. 20. 1–17 Acts 1. 15–end
9 Wednesday	**Mary Sumner, Founder of the Mothers' Union, 1921**			
Gw	Com. Saint *or* *also* Heb. 13. 1–5	Num. 13.1–2, 25 – 14.1, 26–35 Ps. 106. 14–24 Matt. 15. 21–28	Ps. 119. 57–80 Jer. 38. 1–13 Mark 1. 21–28	Ps. *59*; 60; (67) 1 Sam. 20. 18–end Acts 2. 1–21
10 Thursday	**Laurence, Deacon at Rome, Martyr, 258**			
Gr	Com. Martyr *or* *also* 2 Cor. 9. 6–10	Num. 20. 1–13 Ps. 95. 1, 8–end Matt. 16. 13–23	Ps. 56; *57*; (63†) Jer. 38. 14–end Mark 1. 29–end	Ps. 61; *62*; 64 1 Sam. 21.1 – 22.5 Acts 2. 22–36
11 Friday	**Clare of Assisi, Founder of the Minoresses (Poor Clares), 1253** *John Henry Newman, Priest, Tractarian, 1890*			
Gw	Com. Religious *or* *esp.* Song of Sol. 8. 6–7	Deut. 4. 32–40 Ps. 77. 11–end Matt. 16. 24–end	Ps. *51*; 54 Jer. ch. 39 Mark 2. 1–12	Ps. 38 1 Sam. 22. 6–end Acts 2. 37–end
12 Saturday				
G		Deut. 6. 4–13 Ps. 18. 1–2, 48–end Matt. 17. 14–20	Ps. 68 Jer. ch. 40 Mark 2. 13–22	Ps. 65; *66* 1 Sam. ch. 23 Acts 3. 1–10 ct
13 Sunday	**THE TENTH SUNDAY AFTER TRINITY (Proper 14)**			
G	*Track 1* Gen. 37. 1–4, 12–28 Ps. 105. 1–6, 16–22, 45b (or 105. 1–10) Rom. 10. 5–15 Matt. 14. 22–33	*Track 2* 1 Kings 19. 9–18 Ps. 85. 8–13 Rom. 10. 5–15 Matt. 14. 22–33	Ps. 88 Song of Sol. 8. 5–7 *or* 1 Macc. 14. 4–15 2 Pet. 3. 8–13	Ps. 86 1 Kings 11.41 – 12.20 Acts 14. 8–20 *Gospel*: John 6. 35, 41–51

Calendar and Holy Communion	Morning Prayer	Evening Prayer	NOTES

THE TRANSFIGURATION OF OUR LORD (or transferred to 7 August)

w	Exod. 24. 12–end Ps. 84. 1–7 1 John 3. 1–3 Mark 9. 2–7	Ps. 27; 150 Ecclus. 48. 1–10 or 1 Kings 19. 1–16 2 Pet. 1. 16–19	Ps. 72 Exod. 34. 29–end 2 Cor. ch. 3
G	*or, for the Ninth Sunday after Trinity:* Num. 10.35 – 11.3 Ps. 95 1 Cor. 10. 1–13 Luke 16. 1–9 or Luke 15. 11–end	Ps. 85 Song of Sol. 5. 2–end or 1 Macc. 3. 1–12 2 Pet. 1. 1–15	Ps. 80 (or 80. 1–8) 1 Kings 10. 1–13 Acts 13. 1–13 Gospel: John 6. 24–35

For the Transfiguration of Our Lord, see 6 August.
The Name of Jesus

Gw	Jer. 14. 7–9 Ps. 8 Acts 4. 8–12 Matt. 1. 20–23	Jer. 36. 19–end Mark 1. 1–13	1 Sam. 19. 1–18 Acts 1. 1–14
G		Jer. ch. 37 Mark 1. 14–20	1 Sam. 20. 1–17 Acts 1. 15–end
G		Jer. 38. 1–13 Mark 1. 21–28	1 Sam. 20. 18–end Acts 2. 1–21

Laurence, Deacon at Rome, Martyr, 258

Gr	Com. Martyr	Jer. 38. 14–end Mark 1. 29–end	1 Sam. 21.1 – 22.5 Acts 2. 22–36
G		Jer. ch. 39 Mark 2. 1–12	1 Sam. 22. 6–end Acts 2. 37–end
G		Jer. ch. 40 Mark 2. 13–22	1 Sam. ch. 23 Acts 3. 1–10
			ct

THE TENTH SUNDAY AFTER TRINITY

G	Jer. 7. 9–15 Ps. 17. 1–8 1 Cor. 12. 1–11 Luke 19. 41–47a	Ps. 88 Song of Sol. 8. 5–7 or 1 Macc. 14. 4–15 2 Pet. 3. 8–13	Ps. 86 1 Kings 11.41 – 12.20 Acts 14. 8–20

	Sunday Principal Service Weekday Eucharist	Third Service Morning Prayer	Second Service Evening Prayer

14 Monday   *Maximilian Kolbe, Friar, Martyr, 1941*

G **DEL 19**	Deut. 10. 12–end Ps. 147. 13–end Matt. 17. 22–end	Ps. 71 Jer. ch. 41 Mark 2.23 – 3.6	Ps. *72*; 75 1 Sam. ch. 24 Acts 3. 11–end *or First EP of The* *Blessed Virgin Mary* Ps. 72 Prov. 8. 22–31 John 19. 23–27 **W ct**

15 Tuesday   **THE BLESSED VIRGIN MARY***

W	Isa. 61. 10–end *or* Rev. 11.19 – 12.6, 10 Ps. 45. 10–end Gal. 4. 4–7 Luke 1. 46–55	*MP*: Ps. 98; 138; 147. 1–12 Isa. 7. 10–15 Luke 11. 27–28	*EP*: Ps. 132 Song of Sol. 2. 1–7 Acts 1. 6–14
	or, if The Blessed Virgin Mary is celebrated on 8 September:		
G	Deut. 31. 1–8 Ps. 107. 1–3, 42–end *or Canticle*: Deut. 32. 3–4, 7–9 Matt. 18. 1–5, 10, 12–14	Ps. 73 Jer. ch. 42 Mark 3. 7–19a	Ps. 74 1 Sam. ch. 26 Acts 4. 1–12

16 Wednesday

G	Deut. ch. 34 Ps. 66. 14–end Matt. 18. 15–20	Ps. 77 Jer. ch. 43 Mark 3. 19b–end	Ps. 119. 81–104 1 Sam. 28. 3–end Acts 4. 13–31

17 Thursday

G	Josh. 3. 7–11, 13–17 Ps. 114 Matt. 18.21 – 19.1	Ps. 78. 1–39† Jer. 44. 1–14 Mark 4. 1–20	Ps. 78. 40–end† 1 Sam. ch. 31 Acts 4.32 – 5.11

18 Friday

G	Josh. 24. 1–13 Ps. 136. 1–3, 16–22 Matt. 19. 3–12	Ps. 55 Jer. 44. 15–end Mark 4. 21–34	Ps. 69 2 Sam. ch. 1 Acts 5. 12–26

19 Saturday

G	Josh. 24. 14–29 Ps. 16. 1, 5–end Matt. 19. 13–15	Ps. *76*; 79 Jer. ch. 45 Mark 4. 35–end	Ps. 81; *84* 2 Sam. 2. 1–11 Acts 5. 27–end ct

20 Sunday   **THE ELEVENTH SUNDAY AFTER TRINITY (Proper 15)**

G	*Track 1* Gen. 45. 1–15 Ps. 133 Rom. 11. 1–2a, 29–32 Matt. 15. [10–20] 21–28	*Track 2* Isa. 56. 1, 6–8 Ps. 67 Rom. 11. 1–2a, 29–32 Matt. 15. [10–20] 21–28	Ps. 92 Jonah ch. 1 *or* Ecclus. 3. 1–15 2 Pet. 3. 14–end	Ps. 90 (*or* 90. 1–12) 2 Kings 4. 1–37 Acts 16. 1–15 *Gospel*: John 6. 51–58

21 Monday

G **DEL 20**	Judg. 2. 11–19 Ps. 106. 34–42 Matt. 19. 16–22	Ps. *80*; 82 Mic. 1. 1–9 Mark 5. 1–20	Ps. *85*; 86 2 Sam. 3. 12–end Acts ch. 6

*The Blessed Virgin Mary may be celebrated on 8 September instead of 15 August.

Calendar and Holy Communion	Morning Prayer	Evening Prayer	NOTES
G	Jer. ch. 41 Mark 2.23 – 3.6	1 Sam. ch. 24 Acts 3. 11–end	

To celebrate The Blessed Virgin Mary, see *Common Worship* provision.

G	Jer. ch. 42 Mark 3. 7–19a	1 Sam. ch. 26 Acts 4. 1–12	
G	Jer. ch. 43 Mark 3. 19b–end	1 Sam. 28. 3–end Acts 4. 13–31	
G	Jer. 44. 1–14 Mark 4. 1–20	1 Sam. ch. 31 Acts 4.32 – 5.11	
G	Jer. 44. 15–end Mark 4. 21–34	2 Sam. ch. 1 Acts 5. 12–26	
G	Jer. ch. 45 Mark 4. 35–end	2 Sam. 2. 1–11 Acts 5. 27–end	

ct

THE ELEVENTH SUNDAY AFTER TRINITY

G	1 Kings 3. 5–15 Ps. 28 1 Cor. 15. 1–11 Luke 18. 9–14	Ps. 92 Jonah ch. 1 *or* Ecclus. 3. 1–15 2 Pet. 3. 14–end	Ps. 90 (*or* 90. 1–12) 2 Kings 4. 1–37 Acts 16. 1–15	
G		Mic. 1. 1–9 Mark 5. 1–20	2 Sam. 3. 12–end Acts ch. 6	

	Sunday Principal Service Weekday Eucharist	Third Service Morning Prayer	Second Service Evening Prayer
22 Tuesday			
G	Judg. 6. 11–24 Ps. 85. 8–end Matt. 19. 23–end	Ps. 87; **89. 1–18** Mic. ch. 2 Mark 5. 21–34	Ps. 89. 19–end 2 Sam. 5. 1–12 Acts 7. 1–16
23 Wednesday			
G	Judg. 9. 6–15 Ps. 21. 1–6 Matt. 20. 1–16	Ps. 119. 105–128 Mic. ch. 3 Mark 5. 35–end	Ps. **91**; 93 2 Sam. 6. 1–19 Acts 7. 17–43 *or First EP of* *Bartholomew* Ps. 97 Isa. 61. 1–9 2 Cor. 6. 1–10 **R** ct
24 Thursday	**BARTHOLOMEW THE APOSTLE**		
R	Isa. 43. 8–13 *or* Acts 5. 12–16 Ps. 145. 1–7 Acts 5. 12–16 *or* 1 Cor. 4. 9–15 Luke 22. 24–30	*MP*: Ps. 86; 117 Gen. 28. 10–17 John 1. 43–end	*EP*: Ps. 91; 116 Ecclus. 39. 1–10 *or* Deut. 18. 15–19 Matt. 10. 1–22
25 Friday			
G	Ruth 1. 1, 3–6, 14–16, 22 Ps. 146 Matt. 22. 34–40	Ps. **88**; (95) Mic. 5. 2–end Mark 6. 14–29	Ps. 102 2 Sam. 7. 18–end Acts 7.54 – 8.3
26 Saturday			
G	Ruth 2. 1–3, 8–11; 4. 13–17 Ps. 128 Matt. 23. 1–12	Ps. 96; **97**; 100 Mic. ch. 6 Mark 6. 30–44	Ps. 104 2 Sam. ch. 9 Acts 8. 4–25 ct
27 Sunday	**THE TWELFTH SUNDAY AFTER TRINITY (Proper 16)**		
G	*Track 1* Exod. 1.8 – 2.10 Ps. 124 Rom. 12. 1–8 Matt. 16. 13–20	*Track 2* Isa. 51. 1–6 Ps. 138 Rom. 12. 1–8 Matt. 16. 13–20	Ps. 104. 1–25 Jonah ch. 2 *or* Ecclus. 3. 17–29 Rev. ch. 1	Ps. 95 2 Kings 6. 8–23 Acts 17. 15–end *Gospel*: John 6. 56–69
28 Monday	**Augustine, Bishop of Hippo, Teacher, 430**		
Gw DEL 21	Com. Teacher *or* *esp.* Ecclus. 39. 1–10 *also* Rom. 13. 11–13	1 Thess. 1. 1–5, 8–end Ps. 149. 1–5 Matt. 23. 13–22	Ps. **98**; 99; 101 Mic. 7. 1–7 Mark 6. 45–end	Ps. **105**† (*or* 103) 2 Sam. ch. 11. Acts 8. 26–end
29 Tuesday	**The Beheading of John the Baptist**		
Gr	Jer. 1. 4–10 *or* Ps. 11 Heb. 11.32 – 12.2 Matt. 14. 1–12	1 Thess. 2. 1–8 Ps. 139. 1–9 Matt. 23. 23–26	Ps. **106**† (*or* 103) Mic. 7. 8–end Mark 7. 1–13	Ps. 107† 2 Sam. 12. 1–25 Acts 9. 1–19a
30 Wednesday	**John Bunyan, Spiritual Writer, 1688**		
Gw	Com. Teacher *or* *also* Heb. 12. 1–2 Luke 21. 21, 34–36	1 Thess. 2. 9–13 Ps. 126 Matt. 23. 27–32	Ps. 110; **111**; 112 Hab. 1. 1–11 Mark 7. 14–23	Ps. 119. 129–152 2 Sam. 15. 1–12 Acts 9. 19b–31

Calendar and Holy Communion	Morning Prayer	Evening Prayer	NOTES
G	Mic. ch. 2 Mark 5. 21–34	2 Sam. 5. 1–12 Acts 7. 1–16	
G	Mic. ch. 3 Mark 5. 35–end	2 Sam. 6. 1–19 Acts 7. 17–43 *or First EP of* *Bartholomew* (Ps. 97) Isa. 61. 1–9 2 Cor. 6. 1–10 **R ct**	

BARTHOLOMEW THE APOSTLE

Calendar and Holy Communion	Morning Prayer	Evening Prayer	NOTES
R Gen. 28. 10–17 Ps. 15 Acts 5. 12–16 Luke 22. 24–30	(Ps. 86; 117) Isa. 43. 8–13 John 1. 43–end	(Ps. 91; 116) Ecclus. 39. 1–10 *or* Deut. 18. 15–19 Matt. 10. 1–22	
G	Mic. 5. 2–end Mark 6. 14–29	2 Sam. 7. 18–end Acts 7.54 – 8.3	
G	Mic. ch. 6 Mark 6. 30–44	2 Sam. ch. 9 Acts 8. 4–25 **ct**	

THE TWELFTH SUNDAY AFTER TRINITY

Calendar and Holy Communion	Morning Prayer	Evening Prayer	NOTES
G Exod. 34. 29–end Ps. 34. 1–10 2 Cor. 3. 4–9 Mark 7. 31–37	Ps. 104. 1–25 Jonah ch. 2 *or* Ecclus. 3. 17–29 Rev. ch. 1	Ps. 95 2 Kings 6. 8–23 Acts 17. 15–end	

Augustine, Bishop of Hippo, 430

Calendar and Holy Communion	Morning Prayer	Evening Prayer	NOTES
Gw Com. Doctor	Mic. 7. 1–7 Mark 6. 45–end	2 Sam. ch. 11 Acts 8. 26–end	

The Beheading of John the Baptist

Calendar and Holy Communion	Morning Prayer	Evening Prayer	NOTES
Gr 2 Chron. 24. 17–21 Ps. 92. 11–end Heb. 11.32 – 12.2 Matt. 14. 1–12	Mic. 7. 8–end Mark 7. 1–13	2 Sam. 12. 1–25 Acts 9. 1–19a	
G	Hab. 1. 1–11 Mark 7. 14–23	2 Sam. 15. 1–12 Acts 9. 19b–31	

		Sunday Principal Service Weekday Eucharist	Third Service Morning Prayer	Second Service Evening Prayer
31 Thursday	**Aidan, Bishop of Lindisfarne, Missionary, 651**			
Gw	Com. Missionary *or* *also* 1 Cor. 9. 16–19	1 Thess. 3. 7–end Ps. 90. 13–end Matt. 24. 42–end	Ps. 113; **115** Hab. 1.12 – 2.5 Mark 7. 24–30	Ps. 114; **116**; 117 2 Sam. 15. 13–end Acts 9. 32–end

September 2023

		Sunday Principal Service Weekday Eucharist	Third Service Morning Prayer	Second Service Evening Prayer
1 Friday	*Giles of Provence, Hermit, c. 710*			
G		1 Thess. 4. 1–8 Ps. 97 Matt. 25. 1–13	Ps. 139 Hab. 2. 6–end Mark 7. 31–end	Ps. **130**; 131; 137 2 Sam. 16. 1–14 Acts 10. 1–16
2 Saturday	*The Martyrs of Papua New Guinea, 1901 and 1942*			
G		1 Thess. 4. 9–12 Ps. 98. 1–2, 8–end Matt. 25. 14–30	Ps. 120; **121**; 122 Hab. 3. 2–19a Mark 8. 1–10	Ps. 118 2 Sam. 17. 1–23 Acts 10. 17–33 ct
3 Sunday	**THE THIRTEENTH SUNDAY AFTER TRINITY (Proper 17)**			
G	*Track 1* Exod. 3. 1–15 Ps. 105. 1–6, 23–26, 45b *or* Ps. 115 Rom. 12. 9–end Matt. 16. 21–end	*Track 2* Jer. 15. 15–21 Ps. 26. 1–8 Rom. 12. 9–end Matt. 16. 21–end	Ps. 107. 1–32 Jonah 3. 1–9 *or* Ecclus. 11. [7–18] 19–28 Rev. 3. 14–end	Ps. 105. 1–15 2 Kings 6. 24–25; 7. 3–end Acts 18. 1–16 *Gospel*: Mark 7. 1–8, 14–15, 21–23
4 Monday	*Birinus, Bishop of Dorchester (Oxon), Apostle of Wessex, 650**			
G **DEL 22**		1 Thess. 4. 13–end Ps. 96 Luke 4. 16–30	Ps. 123; 124; 125; **126** Hag. 1. 1–11 Mark 8. 11–21	Ps. **127**; 128; 129 2 Sam. 18. 1–18 Acts 10. 34–end
5 Tuesday				
G		1 Thess. 5. 1–6, 9–11 Ps. 27. 1–8 Luke 4. 31–37	Ps. **132**; 133 Hag. 1.12 – 2.9 Mark 8. 22–26	Ps. (134); **135** 2 Sam. 18.19 – 19.8a Acts 11. 1–18
6 Wednesday	*Allen Gardiner, Missionary, Founder of the South American Mission Society, 1851*			
G		Col. 1. 1–8 Ps. 34. 11–18 Luke 4. 38–end	Ps. 119. 153–end Hag. 2. 10–end Mark 8.27 – 9.1	Ps. 136 2 Sam. 19. 8b–23 Acts 11. 19–end
7 Thursday				
G		Col. 1. 9–14 Ps. 98. 1–5 Luke 5. 1–11	Ps. **143**; 146 Zech. 1. 1–17 Mark 9. 2–13	Ps. **138**; 140; 141 2 Sam. 19. 24–end Acts 12. 1–17
8 Friday	**The Birth of the Blessed Virgin Mary****			
Gw	Com. BVM *or*	Col. 1. 15–20 Ps. 89. 19b–28 Luke 5. 33–end	Ps. 142; **144** Zech. 1.18 – 2.end Mark 9. 14–29	Ps. 145 2 Sam. 23. 1–7 Acts 12. 18–end
9 Saturday	*Charles Fuge Lowder, Priest, 1880*			
G		Col. 1. 21–23 Ps. 117 Luke 6. 1–5	Ps. 147 Zech. ch. 3 Mark 9. 30–37	Ps. **148**; 149; 150 2 Sam. ch. 24 Acts 13. 1–12 ct

*Cuthbert may be celebrated on 4 September instead of 20 March.
**The Blessed Virgin Mary may be celebrated on 8 September instead of 15 August.

Calendar and Holy Communion	Morning Prayer	Evening Prayer	NOTES
G	Hab. 1.12 – 2.5 Mark 7. 24–30	2 Sam. 15. 13–end Acts 9. 32–end	
Giles of Provence, Hermit, c. 710			
Gw Com. Abbot	Hab. 2. 6–end Mark 7. 31–end	2 Sam. 16. 1–14 Acts 10. 1–16	
G	Hab. 3. 2–19a Mark 8. 1–10	2 Sam. 17. 1–23 Acts 10. 17–33	
		ct	
THE THIRTEENTH SUNDAY AFTER TRINITY			
G Lev. 19. 13–18 Ps. 74. 20–end Gal. 3. 16–22 or Heb. 13. 1–6 Luke 10. 23b–37	Ps. 107. 1–32 Jonah 3. 1–9 or Ecclus. 11. [7–18] 19–28 Rev. 3. 14–end	Ps. 105. 1–15 2 Kings 6. 24–25; 7. 3–end Acts 18. 1–16	
G	Hag. 1. 1–11 Mark 8. 11–21	2 Sam. 18. 1–18 Acts 10. 34–end	
G	Hag. 1.12 – 2.9 Mark 8. 22–26	2 Sam. 18.19 – 19.8a Acts 11. 1–18	
G	Hag. 2. 10–end Mark 8.27 – 9.1	2 Sam. 19. 8b–23 Acts 11. 19–end	
Evurtius, Bishop of Orleans, 4th century			
Gw Com. Bishop	Zech. 1. 1–17 Mark 9. 2–13	2 Sam. 19. 24–end Acts 12. 1–17	
The Nativity of the Blessed Virgin Mary			
Gw Gen. 3. 9–15 Ps. 45. 11–18 Rom. 5. 12–17 Luke 11. 27–28	Zech. 1.18 – 2.end Mark 9. 14–29	2 Sam. 23. 1–7 Acts 12. 18–end	
G	Zech. ch. 3 Mark 9. 30–37	2 Sam. ch. 24 Acts 13. 1–12	
		ct	

		Sunday Principal Service Weekday Eucharist	Third Service Morning Prayer	Second Service Evening Prayer
10 Sunday	**THE FOURTEENTH SUNDAY AFTER TRINITY (Proper 18)**			
G	*Track 1* Exod. 12. 1–14 Ps. 149 Rom. 13. 8–end Matt. 18. 15–20	*Track 2* Ezek. 33. 7–11 Ps. 119. 33–40 Rom. 13. 8–end Matt. 18. 15–20	Ps. 119. 17–32 Jonah 3.10 – 4.11 or Ecclus. 27.30 – 28.9 Rev. 8. 1–5	Ps. 108; [115] Ezek. 12.21 – 13.16 Acts 19. 1–20 *Gospel:* Mark 7. 24–end
11 Monday				
G **DEL 23**		Col. 1.24 – 2.3 Ps. 62. 1–7 Luke 6. 6–11	Ps. *1*; 2; 3 Zech. ch. 4 Mark 9. 38–end	Ps. *4*; 7 1 Kings 1. 5–31 Acts 13. 13–43
12 Tuesday				
G		Col. 2. 6–15 Ps. 8 Luke 6. 12–19	Ps. *5*; 6; (8) Zech. 6. 9–end Mark 10. 1–16	Ps. *9*; 10† 1 Kings 1.32 – 2.4, 10–12 Acts 13.44 – 14.7
13 Wednesday	**John Chrysostom, Bishop of Constantinople, Teacher, 407**			
Gw	Com. Teacher *or* *esp.* Matt. 5. 13–19 *also* Jer. 1. 4–10	Col. 3. 1–11 Ps. 15 Luke 6. 20–26	Ps. 119. 1–32 Zech. ch. 7 Mark 10. 17–31	Ps. *11*; 12; 13 1 Kings ch. 3 Acts 14. 8–end *or First EP of Holy* *Cross Day* Ps. 66 Isa. 52.13 – 53.end Eph. 2. 11–end **R ct**
14 Thursday	**HOLY CROSS DAY**			
R		Num. 21. 4–9 Ps. 22. 23–28 Phil. 2. 6–11 John 3. 13–17	*MP*: Ps. 2; 8; 146 Gen. 3. 1–15 John 12. 27–36a	*EP*: Ps. 110; 150 Isa. 63. 1–16 1 Cor. 1. 18–25
15 Friday	**Cyprian, Bishop of Carthage, Martyr, 258**			
Gr	Com. Martyr *or* *esp.* 1 Pet. 4. 12–end *also* Matt. 18. 18–22	1 Tim. 1. 1–2, 12–14 Ps. 16 Luke 6. 39–42	Ps. 17; *19* Zech. 8. 9–end Mark 10. 35–45	Ps. 22 1 Kings 6. 1, 11–28 Acts 15. 22–35
16 Saturday	**Ninian, Bishop of Galloway, Apostle of the Picts, c. 432** *Edward Bouverie Pusey, Priest, Tractarian, 1882*			
Gw	Com. Missionary *or* *esp.* Acts 13. 46–49 Mark 16. 15–end	1 Tim. 1. 15–17 Ps. 113 Luke 6. 43–end	Ps. 20; 21; *23* Zech. 9. 1–12 Mark 10. 46–end	Ps. *24*; 25 1 Kings 8. 1–30 Acts 15.36 – 16.5 ct
17 Sunday	**THE FIFTEENTH SUNDAY AFTER TRINITY (Proper 19)**			
G	*Track 1* Exod. 14. 19–end Ps. 114 or *Canticle:* Exod. 15. 1b–11, 20–21 Rom. 14. 1–12 Matt. 18. 21–35	*Track 2* Gen. 50. 15–21 Ps. 103. 1–13 (or 103. 8–13) Rom. 14. 1–12 Matt. 18. 21–35	Ps. 119. 65–88 Isa. 44.24 – 45.8 Rev. 12. 1–12	Ps. 119. 41–48 [49–64] Ezek. 20. 1–8, 33–44 Acts 20. 17–end *Gospel:* Mark 8. 27–end

Calendar and Holy Communion	Morning Prayer	Evening Prayer	NOTES

THE FOURTEENTH SUNDAY AFTER TRINITY

G 2 Kings 5. 9–16 Ps. 118. 1–9 Gal. 5. 16–24 Luke 17. 11–19	Ps. 119. 17–32 Jonah 3.10 – 4.11 or Ecclus. 27.30 – 28.9 Rev. 8. 1–5	Ps. 108; [115] Ezek. 12.21 – 13.16 Mark 7. 24–30	
G	Zech. ch. 4 Mark 9. 38–end	1 Kings 1. 5–31 Acts 13. 13–43	
G	Zech. 6. 9–end Mark 10. 1–16	1 Kings 1.32 – 2.4, 10–12 Acts 13.44 – 14.7	
G	Zech. ch. 7 Mark 10. 17–31	1 Kings ch. 3 Acts 14. 8–end	

Holy Cross Day
To celebrate Holy Cross as a festival, see *Common Worship* provision.

Gr Num. 21. 4–9 Ps. 67 1 Cor. 1. 17–25 John 12. 27–33	Zech. 8. 1–8 Mark 10. 32–34	1 Kings 4.29 – 5.12 Acts 15. 1–21	
G	Zech. 8. 9–end Mark 10. 35–45	1 Kings 6. 1, 11–28 Acts 15. 22–35	
G	Zech. 9. 1–12 Mark 10. 46–end	1 Kings 8. 1–30 Acts 15.36 – 16.5	
		ct	

THE FIFTEENTH SUNDAY AFTER TRINITY

G Josh. 24. 14–25 Ps. 92. 1–6 Gal. 6. 11–end Matt. 6. 24–end	Ps. 119. 65–88 Isa. 44.24 – 45.8 Rev. 12. 1–12	Ps. 119. 41–48 [49–64] Ezek. 20. 1–8, 33–44 Acts 20. 17–end	

		Sunday Principal Service Weekday Eucharist	Third Service Morning Prayer	Second Service Evening Prayer
18 Monday				
G **DEL 24**		1 Tim. 2. 1–8 Ps. 28 Luke 7. 1–10	Ps. 27; ***30*** Zech. ch. 10 Mark 11. 1–11	Ps. 26; ***28***; 29 1 Kings 8. 31–62 Acts 16. 6–24
19 Tuesday	*Theodore of Tarsus, Archbishop of Canterbury, 690*			
G		1 Tim. 3. 1–13 Ps. 101 Luke 7. 11–17	Ps. 32; ***36*** Zech. 11. 4–end Mark 11. 12–26	Ps. 33 1 Kings 8.63 – 9.9 Acts 16. 25–end
20 Wednesday	**John Coleridge Patteson, first Bishop of Melanesia and his Companions, Martyrs, 1871**			
Gr	Com. Martyr *or* *esp.* 2 Chron. 24. 17–21 *also* Acts 7. 55–end	1 Tim. 3. 14–end Ps. 111. 1–5 Luke 7. 31–35	Ps. 34 Zech. 12. 1–10 Mark 11. 27–end	Ps. 119. 33–56 1 Kings 10. 1–25 Acts 17. 1–15 *or First EP of Matthew* Ps. 34 Isa. 33. 13–17 Matt. 6. 19–end **R ct**
21 Thursday	**MATTHEW, APOSTLE AND EVANGELIST**			
R		Prov. 3. 13–18 Ps. 119. 65–72 2 Cor. 4. 1–6 Matt. 9. 9–13	*MP*: Ps. 49; 117 1 Kings 19. 15–end 2 Tim. 3. 14–end	*EP*: Ps. 119. 33–40, 89–96 Eccles. 5. 4–12 Matt. 19. 16–end
22 Friday				
G		1 Tim. 6. 2b–12 Ps. 49. 1–9 Luke 8. 1–3	Ps. 31 Zech. 14. 1–11 Mark 12. 13–17	Ps. 35 1 Kings 11. 26–end Acts 18. 1–21
23 Saturday				
G		1 Tim. 6. 13–16 Ps. 100 Luke 8. 4–15	Ps. 41; ***42***; 43 Zech. 14. 12–end Mark 12. 18–27	Ps. 45; ***46*** 1 Kings 12. 1–24 Acts 18.22 – 19.7 **ct**
24 Sunday	**THE SIXTEENTH SUNDAY AFTER TRINITY (Proper 20)**			
G	*Track 1* Exod. 16. 2–15 Ps. 105. 1–6, 37–end (*or* 105. 37–end) Phil. 1. 21–end Matt. 20. 1–16	*Track 2* Jonah 3.10 – 4.end Ps. 145. 1–8 Phil. 1. 21–end Matt. 20. 1–16	Ps. 119. 153–end Isa. 45. 9–22 Rev. 14. 1–5	Ps. 119. 113–136 (*or* 119. 121–128) Ezek. 33.23, 30 – 34.10 Acts 26. 1, 9–25 *Gospel*: Mark 9. 30–37
25 Monday	**Lancelot Andrewes, Bishop of Winchester, Spiritual Writer, 1626** *Sergei of Radonezh, Russian Monastic Reformer, Teacher, 1392*			
Gw **DEL 25**	Com. Bishop *or* *esp.* Isa. 6. 1–8	Ezra 1. 1–6 Ps. 126 Luke 8. 16–18	Ps. 44 Ecclus. 1. 1–10 *or* Ezek. 1. 1–14 Mark 12. 28–34	Ps. ***47***; 49 1 Kings 12.25 – 13.10 Acts 19. 8–20
26 Tuesday	*Wilson Carlile, Founder of the Church Army, 1942*			
G		Ezra 6. 7–8, 12, 14–20 Ps. 124 Luke 8. 19–21	Ps. ***48***; 52 Ecclus. 1. 11–end *or* Ezek. 1.15 – 2.2 Mark 12. 35–end	Ps. 50 1 Kings 13. 11–end Acts 19. 21–end

Calendar and Holy Communion	Morning Prayer	Evening Prayer	NOTES
G	Zech. ch. 10 Mark 11. 1–11	1 Kings 8. 31–62 Acts 16. 6–24	
G	Zech. 11. 4–end Mark 11. 12–26	1 Kings 8.63 – 9.9 Acts 16. 25–end	
G	Zech. 12. 1–10 Mark 11. 27–end	1 Kings 10. 1–25 Acts 17. 1–15 or First EP of Matthew (Ps. 34) Prov. 3. 3–18 Matt. 6. 19–end	
		R ct	

MATTHEW, APOSTLE AND EVANGELIST

R	Isa. 33. 13–17 Ps. 119. 65–72 2 Cor. 4. 1–6 Matt. 9. 9–13	(Ps. 49; 117) 1 Kings 19. 15–end 2 Tim. 3. 14–end	(Ps. 119. 33–40, 89–96) Eccles. 5. 4–12 Matt. 19. 16–end
G		Zech. 14. 1–11 Mark 12. 13–17	1 Kings 11. 26–end Acts 18. 1–21
G		Zech. 14. 12–end Mark 12. 18–27	1 Kings 12. 1–24 Acts 18.22 – 19.7
			ct

THE SIXTEENTH SUNDAY AFTER TRINITY

G	1 Kings 17. 17–end Ps. 102. 12–17 Eph. 3. 13–end Luke 7. 11–17	Ps. 119. 153–end Isa. 45. 9–22 Rev. 14. 1–5	Ps. 119. 113–136 (or 119. 121–128) Ezek. 33.23, 30 – 34.10 Acts 26. 1, 9–25
G		Ecclus. 1. 1–10 or Ezek. 1. 1–14 Mark 12. 28–34	1 Kings 12.25 – 13.10 Acts 19. 8–20

Cyprian, Bishop of Carthage, Martyr, 258

Gr	Com. Martyr	Ecclus. 1. 11–end or Ezek. 1.15 – 2.2 Mark 12. 35–end	1 Kings 13. 11–end Acts 19. 21–end

	Sunday Principal Service Weekday Eucharist	Third Service Morning Prayer	Second Service Evening Prayer

27 Wednesday   Vincent de Paul, Founder of the Congregation of the Mission (Lazarists), 1660
Ember Day*

Gw *or* **Rw**	Com. Religious *or* *also* 1 Cor. 1. 25–end Matt. 25. 34–40	Ezra 9. 5–9 *Canticle*: Song of Tobit *or* Ps. 103. 1–6 Luke 9. 1–6	Ps. 119. 57–80 Ecclus. ch. 2 *or* Ezek. 2.3 – 3.11 Mark 13. 1–13	Ps. **59**; 60; (67) 1 Kings ch. 17 Acts 20. 1–16

28 Thursday

G		Hag. 1. 1–8 Ps. 149. 1–5 Luke 9. 7–9	Ps. 56; **57**; (63†) Ecclus. 3. 17–29 *or* Ezek. 3. 12–end Mark 13. 14–23	Ps. 61; **62**; 64 1 Kings 18. 1–20 Acts 20. 17–end *or First EP of Michael and All Angels* Ps. 91 2 Kings 6. 8–17 Matt. 18. 1–6, 10 **W ct**

29 Friday   **MICHAEL AND ALL ANGELS**
Ember Day*

W		Gen. 28. 10–17 *or* Rev. 12. 7–12 Ps. 103. 19–end Rev. 12. 7–12 *or* Heb. 1. 5–end John 1. 47–end	*MP*: Ps. 34; 150 Tob. 12. 6–end *or* Dan. 12. 1–4 Acts 12. 1–11	*EP*: Ps. 138; 148 Dan. 10. 4–end Rev. ch. 5

30 Saturday   Ember Day*
Jerome, Translator of the Scriptures, Teacher, 420

G *or* R		Zech. 2. 1–5, 10–11 Ps. 125 *or Canticle*: Jer. 31. 10–13 Luke 9. 43b–45	Ps. 68 Ecclus. 4.29 – 6.1 *or* Ezek. ch. 9 Mark 13. 32–end	Ps. 65; **66** 1 Kings ch. 19 Acts 21. 17–36 **ct** *or First EP of Dedication Festival* Ps. 24 2 Chron. 7. 11–16 John 4. 19–29 **𝖂 ct**

October 2023

1 Sunday   **THE SEVENTEENTH SUNDAY AFTER TRINITY (Proper 21)**

G		*Track 1* Exod. 17. 1–7 Ps. 78. 1–4, 12–16 (*or* 78. 1–7) Phil. 2. 1–13 Matt. 21. 23–32 *or, if observed as Dedication Festival*:	*Track 2* Ezek. 18. 1–4, 25–end Ps. 25. 1–8 Phil. 2. 1–13 Matt. 21. 23–32	Ps. 125; 126; 127 Isa. 48. 12–21 Luke 11. 37–54	Ps. [120; 123]; 124 Ezek. 37. 15–end 1 John 2. 22–end *Gospel*: Mark 9. 38–end
𝖂		1 Kings 8. 22–30 *or* Rev. 21. 9–14 Ps. 122 Heb. 12. 18–24 Matt. 21. 12–16	*MP*: Ps. 48; 150 Hag. 2. 6–9 Heb. 10. 19–25	*EP*: Ps. 132 Jer. 7. 1–11 1 Cor. 3. 9–17 *Gospel*: Luke 19. 1–10

*For Ember Day provision, see p. 11.

Calendar and Holy Communion	Morning Prayer	Evening Prayer	NOTES
Ember Day			

G Ember CEG	Ecclus. ch. 2 *or* Ezek. 2.3 – 3.11 Mark 13. 1–13	1 Kings ch. 17 Acts 20. 1–16	

G	Ecclus. 3. 17–29 *or* Ezek. 3. 12–end Mark 13. 14–23	1 Kings 18. 1–20 Acts 20. 17–end *or First EP of Michael and All Angels* (Ps. 91) 2 Kings 6. 8–17 John 1. 47–51	
		W ct	

MICHAEL AND ALL ANGELS
Ember Day

W	Dan. 10. 10–19a Ps. 103. 17–22 Rev. 12. 7–12 Matt. 18. 1–10	(Ps. 34; 150) Tob. 12. 6–end *or* Dan. 12. 1–4 Acts 12. 1–11	(Ps. 138; 148) Gen. 28. 10–17 Rev. ch. 5	

Jerome, Translator of the Scriptures, Teacher, 420
Ember Day

Gw Com. Doctor *or* Ember CEG	Ecclus. 4.29 – 6.1 *or* Ezek. ch. 9 Mark 13. 32–end	1 Kings ch. 19 Acts 21. 17–36 **ct** *or First EP of Dedication Festival* Ps. 24 2 Chron. 7. 11–16 John 4. 19–29	
		𝔚 ct	

THE SEVENTEENTH SUNDAY AFTER TRINITY

G	Prov. 25. 6–14 Ps. 33. 6–12 Eph. 4. 1–6 Luke 14. 1–11	Ps. 125; 126; 127 Isa. 48. 12–21 Luke 11. 37–54	Ps. [120; 123]; 124 Ezek. 37. 15–end 1 John 2. 22–end	

or, if observed as Dedication Festival:			
𝔚 2 Chron. 7. 11–16 Ps. 122 1 Cor. 3. 9–17 *or* 1 Pet. 2. 1–5 Matt. 21. 12–16 *or* John 10. 22–29	Ps. 48; 150 Hag. 2. 6–9 Heb. 10. 19–25	Ps. 132 Jer. 7. 1–11 Luke 19. 1–10	

		Sunday Principal Service / Weekday Eucharist	Third Service / Morning Prayer	Second Service / Evening Prayer

2 Monday

| G
DEL 26 | | Zech. 8. 1–8
Ps. 102. 12–22
Luke 9. 46–50 | Ps. 71
Ecclus. 6. 14–end
or Ezek. 10. 1–19
Mark 14. 1–11 | Ps. **72**; 75
1 Kings ch. 21
Acts 21.37 – 22.21 |

3 Tuesday   *George Bell, Bishop of Chichester, Ecumenist, Peacemaker, 1958*

| G | | Zech. 8. 20–end
Ps. 87
Luke 9. 51–56 | Ps. 73
Ecclus. 7. 27–end
or Ezek. 11. 14–end
Mark 14. 12–25 | Ps. 74
1 Kings 22. 1–28
Acts 22.22 – 23.11 |

4 Wednesday   Francis of Assisi, Friar, Deacon, Founder of the Friars Minor, 1226

| Gw | Com. Religious   *or*
also Gal. 6. 14–end
Luke 12. 22–34 | Neh. 2. 1–8
Ps. 137. 1–6
Luke 9. 57–end | Ps. 77
Ecclus. 10. 6–8, 12–24
or Ezek. 12. 1–16
Mark 14. 26–42 | Ps. 119. 81–104
1 Kings 22. 29–45
Acts 23. 12–end |

5 Thursday

| G | | Neh. 8. 1–12
Ps. 19. 7–11
Luke 10. 1–12 | Ps. 78. 1–39†
Ecclus. 11. 7–28
or Ezek. 12. 17–end
Mark 14. 43–52 | Ps. 78. 40–end†
2 Kings 1. 2–17
Acts 24. 1–23 |

6 Friday   William Tyndale, Translator of the Scriptures, Reformation Martyr, 1536

| Gr | Com. Martyr   *or*
also Prov. 8. 4–11
2 Tim. 3. 12–end | Baruch 1. 15–end
or Deut. 31. 7–13
Ps. 79. 1–9
Luke 10. 13–16 | Ps. 55
Ecclus. 14.20 – 15.10
or Ezek. 13. 1–16
Mark 14. 53–65 | Ps. 69
2 Kings 2. 1–18
Acts 24.24 – 25.12 |

7 Saturday

| G | | Baruch 4. 5–12, 27–29
or Josh. 22. 1–6
Ps. 69. 33–37
Luke 10. 17–24 | Ps. **76**; 79
Ecclus. 15. 11–end
or Ezek. 14. 1–11
Mark 14. 66–end | Ps. 81; **84**
2 Kings 4. 1–37
Acts 25. 13–end
ct |

8 **Sunday**   THE EIGHTEENTH SUNDAY AFTER TRINITY (Proper 22)

| G | *Track 1*
Exod. 20. 1–4, 7–9,
12–20
Ps. 19 (*or* 19. 7–end)
Phil. 3. 4b–14
Matt. 21. 33–end | *Track 2*
Isa. 5. 1–7
Ps. 80. 9–17
Phil. 3. 4b–14
Matt. 21. 33–end | Ps. 128; 129; 134
Isa. 49. 13–23
Luke 12. 1–12 | Ps. 136 (*or* 136. 1–9)
Prov. 2. 1–11
1 John 2. 1–17
Gospel: Mark 10. 2–16 |

9 Monday   *Denys, Bishop of Paris, and his Companions, Martyrs, c. 250; Robert Grosseteste, Bishop of Lincoln,*
Philosopher, Scientist, 1253

| G
DEL 27 | | Jonah 1.1 – 2.2, 10
Canticle: Jonah
2. 2–4, 7
or Ps. 69. 1–6
Luke 10. 25–37 | Ps. **80**; 82
Ecclus. 16. 17–end
or Ezek. 14. 12–end
Mark 15. 1–15 | Ps. **85**; 86
2 Kings ch. 5
Acts 26. 1–23 |

10 Tuesday   Paulinus, Bishop of York, Missionary, 644
Thomas Traherne, Poet, Spiritual Writer, 1674

| Gw | Com. Missionary   *or*
esp. Matt. 28. 16–end | Jonah ch. 3
Ps. 130
Luke 10. 38–end | Ps. 87; **89. 1–18**
Ecclus. 17. 1–24
or Ezek. 18. 1–20
Mark 15. 16–32 | Ps. 89. 19–end
2 Kings 6. 1–23
Acts 26. 24–end |

	Calendar and Holy Communion	Morning Prayer	Evening Prayer	NOTES
G		Ecclus. 6. 14–end or Ezek. 10. 1–19 Mark 14. 1–11	1 Kings ch. 21 Acts 21.37 – 22.21	
G		Ecclus. 7. 27–end or Ezek. 11. 14–end Mark 14. 12–25	1 Kings 22. 1–28 Acts 22.22 – 23.11	
G		Ecclus. 10. 6–8, 12–24 or Ezek. 12. 1–16 Mark 14. 26–42	1 Kings 22. 29–45 Acts 23. 12–end	
G		Ecclus. 11. 7–28 or Ezek. 12. 17–end Mark 14. 43–52	2 Kings 1. 2–17 Acts 24. 1–23	

Faith of Aquitaine, Martyr, c. 304

	Calendar and Holy Communion	Morning Prayer	Evening Prayer	NOTES
Gr	Com. Virgin Martyr	Ecclus. 14.20 – 15.10 or Ezek. 13. 1–16 Mark 14. 53–65	2 Kings 2. 1–18 Acts 24.24 – 25.12	
G		Ecclus. 15. 11–end or Ezek. 14. 1–11 Mark 14. 66–end	Ps. 81; **84** 2 Kings 4. 1–37 Acts 25. 13–end ct	

THE EIGHTEENTH SUNDAY AFTER TRINITY

	Calendar and Holy Communion	Morning Prayer	Evening Prayer	NOTES
G	Deut. 6. 4–9 Ps. 122 1 Cor. 1. 4–8 Matt. 22. 34–end	Ps. 128; 129; 134 Isa. 49. 13–23 Luke 12. 1–12	Ps. 136 (or 136. 1–9) Prov. 2. 1–11 1 John 2. 1–17	

Denys, Bishop of Paris, Martyr, c. 250

	Calendar and Holy Communion	Morning Prayer	Evening Prayer	NOTES
Gr	Com. Martyr	Ecclus. 16. 17–end or Ezek. 14. 12–end Mark 15. 1–15	2 Kings ch. 5 Acts 26. 1–23	
G		Ecclus. 17. 1–24 or Ezek. 18. 1–20 Mark 15. 16–32	2 Kings 6. 1–23 Acts 26. 24–end	

	Sunday Principal Service / Weekday Eucharist	Third Service / Morning Prayer	Second Service / Evening Prayer

11 Wednesday *Ethelburga, Abbess of Barking, 675; James the Deacon, Companion of Paulinus, 7th century*

G	Jonah ch. 4	Ps. *91*; 93	Ps. *91*; 93
	Ps. 86. 1–9	Ecclus. 18. 1–14	2 Kings 9. 1–16
	Luke 11. 1–4	or Ezek. 18. 21–32	Acts 27. 1–26
		Mark 15. 33–41	

Correction: Third Service Ps. is "Ps. 119. 105–128" and Ecclus reads as above.

12 Thursday **Wilfrid of Ripon, Bishop, Missionary, 709**
Elizabeth Fry, Prison Reformer, 1845; Edith Cavell, Nurse, 1915

Gw	Com. Missionary *or* Mal. 3.13 – 4.2a	Ps. 90; *92*	Ps. 94
	esp. Luke 5. 1–11 Ps. 1	Ecclus. 19. 4–17	2 Kings 9. 17–end
	also 1 Cor. 1. 18–25 Luke 11. 5–13	or Ezek. 20. 1–20	Acts 27. 27–end
		Mark 15. 42–end	

13 Friday **Edward the Confessor, King of England, 1066**

Gw	Com. Saint *or* Joel 1. 13–15; 2. 1–2	Ps. *88*; (95)	Ps. 102
	also 2 Sam. 23. 1–5 Ps. 9. 1–7	Ecclus. 19. 20–end	2 Kings 12. 1–19
	1 John 4. 13–16 Luke 11. 15–26	or Ezek. 20. 21–38	Acts 28. 1–16
		Mark 16. 1–8	

14 Saturday

G	Joel 3. 12–end	Ps. 96; *97*; 100	Ps. 104
	Ps. 97. 1, 8–end	Ecclus. 21. 1–17	2 Kings 17. 1–23
	Luke 11. 27–28	or Ezek. 24. 15–end	Acts 28. 17–end
		Mark 16. 9–end	**ct**

15 Sunday **THE NINETEENTH SUNDAY AFTER TRINITY (Proper 23)**

G	*Track 1* *Track 2*	Ps. 138; 141	Ps. 139. 1–18
	Exod. 32. 1–14 Isa. 25. 1–9	Isa. 50. 4–10	(or 139. 1–11)
	Ps. 106. 1–6, 19–23 Ps. 23	Luke 13. 22–30	Prov. 3. 1–18
	(or 106. 1–6)		1 John 3. 1–15
	Phil. 4. 1–9 Phil. 4. 1–9		*Gospel:* Mark 10. 17–31
	Matt. 22. 1–14 Matt. 22. 1–14		

16 Monday *Nicholas Ridley, Bishop of London, and Hugh Latimer, Bishop of Worcester, Reformation Martyrs, 1555*

G	Rom. 1. 1–7	Ps. *98*; 99; 101	Ps. *105*† (or 103)
DEL 28	Ps. 98	Ecclus. 22. 6–22	2 Kings 17. 24–end
	Luke 11. 29–32	or Ezek. 28. 1–19	Phil. 1. 1–11
		John 13. 1–11	

17 Tuesday **Ignatius, Bishop of Antioch, Martyr, c. 107**

Gr	Com. Martyr *or* Rom. 1. 16–25	Ps. *106*†; (or 103)	Ps. 107†
	also Phil. 3. 7–12 Ps. 19. 1–4	Ecclus. 22.27 – 23.15	2 Kings 18. 1–12
	John 6. 52–58 Luke 11. 37–41	or Ezek. 33. 1–20	Phil. 1. 12–end
		John 13. 12–20	or *First EP of Luke*
			Ps. 33
			Hos. 6. 1–3
			2 Tim. 3. 10–end
			R ct

18 Wednesday **LUKE THE EVANGELIST**

R	Isa. 35. 3–6	*MP:* Ps. 145; 146	*EP:* Ps. 103
	or Acts 16. 6–12a	Isa. ch. 55	Ecclus. 38. 1–14
	Ps. 147. 1–7	Luke 1. 1–4	or Isa. 61. 1–6
	2 Tim. 4. 5–17		Col. 4. 7–end
	Luke 10. 1–9		

Calendar and Holy Communion	Morning Prayer	Evening Prayer	NOTES
G	Ecclus. 18. 1–14 *or* Ezek. 18. 21–32 Mark 15. 33–41	2 Kings 9. 1–16 Acts 27. 1–26	
G	Ecclus. 19. 4–17 *or* Ezek. 20. 1–20 Mark 15. 42–end	2 Kings 9. 17–end Acts 27. 27–end	
Edward the Confessor, King of England, 1066, translated 1163			
Gw Com. Saint	Ecclus. 19. 20–end *or* Ezek. 20. 21–38 Mark 16. 1–8	2 Kings 12. 1–19 Acts 28. 1–16	
G	Ecclus. 21. 1–17 *or* Ezek. 24. 15–end Mark 16. 9–end	2 Kings 17. 1–23 Acts 28. 17–end **ct**	
NINETEENTH SUNDAY AFTER TRINITY			
G Gen. 18. 23–32 Ps. 141. 1–9 Eph. 4. 17–end Matt. 9. 1–8	Ps. 138; 141 Isa. 50. 4–10 Luke 13. 22–30	Ps. 139. 1–18 (*or* 139. 1–11) Prov. 3. 1–18 1 John 3. 1–15	
G	Ecclus. 22. 6–22 *or* Ezek. 28. 1–19 John 13. 1–11	2 Kings 17. 24–end Phil. 1. 1–11	
Etheldreda, Abbess of Ely, 679			
Gw Com. Abbess	Ecclus. 22.27 – 23.15 *or* Ezek. 33. 1–20 John 13. 12–20	2 Kings 18. 1–12 Phil. 1. 12–end *or First EP of Luke* (Ps. 33) Hos. 6. 1–3 2 Tim. 3. 10–end **R ct**	
LUKE THE EVANGELIST			
R Isa. 35. 3–6 Ps. 147. 1–6 2 Tim. 4. 5–15 Luke 10. 1–9 *or* Luke 7. 36–end	(Ps. 145; 146) Isa. ch. 55 Luke 1. 1–4	(Ps. 103) Ecclus. 38. 1–14 *or* Isa. 61. 1–6 Col. 4. 7–end	

	Sunday Principal Service Weekday Eucharist	Third Service Morning Prayer	Second Service Evening Prayer

19 Thursday — Henry Martyn, Translator of the Scriptures, Missionary in India and Persia, 1812

Gw	Com. Missionary *or* Rom. 3. 21–30 *esp.* Mark 16. 15–end	Ps. 113; *115* Ecclus. 24. 23–end	Ps. 114; *116*; 117 2 Kings 19. 1–19
	also Isa. 55. 6–11	Ps. 130	*or* Ezek. 34. 1–16	Phil. 2. 14–end
		Luke 11. 47–end	John 13. 31–end	

20 Friday

G	Rom. 4. 1–8	Ps. 139	Ps. *130*; 131; 137
	Ps. 32	Ecclus. 27.30 – 28.9	2 Kings 19. 20–36
	Luke 12. 1–7	*or* Ezek. 34. 17–end	Phil. 3.1 – 4.1
		John 14. 1–14	

21 Saturday

G	Rom. 4. 13, 16–18	Ps. 120; *121*; 122	Ps. 118
	Ps. 105. 6–10, 41–44	Ecclus. 28. 14–end	2 Kings ch. 20
	Luke 12. 8–12	*or* Ezek. 36. 16–36	Phil. 4. 2–end
		John 14. 15–end	ct

22 Sunday — **TWENTIETH SUNDAY AFTER TRINITY (Proper 24)**

G	*Track 1*	*Track 2*	Ps. 145; 149	Ps. 142 [143. 1–11]
	Exod. 33. 12–end	Isa. 45. 1–7	Isa. 54. 1–14	Prov. 4. 1–18
	Ps. 99	Ps. 96. 1–9 [10–13]	Luke 13. 31–end	1 John 3.16 – 4.6
	1 Thess. 1. 1–10	1 Thess. 1. 1–10		*Gospel:* Mark 10. 35–45
	Matt. 22. 15–22	Matt. 22. 15–22		

23 Monday

G **DEL 29**	Rom. 4. 20–end *Canticle:* Benedictus	Ps. 123; 124; 125; *126* Ecclus. 31. 1–11	Ps. *127*; 128; 129 2 Kings 21. 1–18
	1–6	*or* Ezek. 37. 1–14	1 Tim. 1. 1–17
	Luke 12. 13–21	John 15. 1–11	

24 Tuesday

G	Rom. 5. 12, 15, 17–end	Ps. *132*; 133	Ps. (134); *135*
	Ps. 40. 7–12	Ecclus. 34. 9–end	2 Kings 22.1 – 23.3
	Luke 12. 35–38	*or* Ezek. 37. 15–end	1 Tim. 1.18 – 2.end
		John 15. 12–17	

25 Wednesday — *Crispin and Crispinian, Martyrs at Rome, c. 287*

G	Rom. 6. 12–18	Ps. 119. 153–end	Ps. 136
	Ps. 124	Ecclus. ch. 35	2 Kings 23. 4–25
	Luke 12. 39–48	*or* Ezek. 39. 21–end	1 Tim. ch. 3
		John 15. 18–end	

26 Thursday — **Alfred the Great, King of the West Saxons, Scholar, 899**
Cedd, Abbot of Lastingham, Bishop of the East Saxons, 664*

Gw	Com. Saint *or* Rom. 6. 19–end	Ps. *143*; 146	Ps. *138*; 140; 141
	also 2 Sam. 23. 1–5	Ps. 1	Ecclus. 37. 7–24	2 Kings 23.36 – 24.17
	John 18. 33–37	Luke 12. 49–53	*or* Ezek. 43. 1–12	1 Tim. ch. 4
			John 16. 1–15	

*Chad may be celebrated with Cedd on 26 October instead of 2 March.

	Calendar and Holy Communion	Morning Prayer	Evening Prayer	NOTES
G		Ecclus. 24. 23–end or Ezek. 34. 1–16 John 13. 31–end	2 Kings 19. 1–19 Phil. 2. 14–end	
G		Ecclus. 27.30 – 28.9 or Ezek. 34. 17–end John 14. 1–14	2 Kings 19. 20–36 Phil. 3.1 – 4.1	
G		Ecclus. 28. 14–end or Ezek. 36. 16–36 John 14. 15–end	2 Kings ch. 20 Phil. 4. 2–end ct	

TWENTIETH SUNDAY AFTER TRINITY

	Calendar and Holy Communion	Morning Prayer	Evening Prayer	NOTES
G	Prov. 9. 1–6 Ps. 145. 15–end Eph. 5. 15–21 Matt. 22. 1–14	Ps. 138 Isa. 54. 1–14 Luke 13. 31–end	Ps. 142 [143. 1–11] Prov. 4. 1–18 1 John 3.16 – 4.6	
G		Ecclus. 31. 1–11 or Ezek. 37. 1–14 John 15. 1–11	2 Kings 21. 1–18 1 Tim. 1. 1–17	
G		Ecclus. 34. 9–end or Ezek. 37. 15–end John 15. 12–17	2 Kings 22.1 – 23.3 1 Tim. 1.18 – 2.end	

Crispin, Martyr at Rome, c. 287

	Calendar and Holy Communion	Morning Prayer	Evening Prayer	NOTES
Gr	Com. Martyr	Ecclus. ch. 35 or Ezek. 39. 21–end John 15. 18–end	2 Kings 23. 4–25 1 Tim. ch. 3	
G		Ecclus. 37. 7–24 or Ezek. 43. 1–12 John 16. 1–15	2 Kings 23.36 – 24.17 1 Tim. ch. 4	

		Sunday Principal Service Weekday Eucharist	Third Service Morning Prayer	Second Service Evening Prayer

27 Friday

G		Rom. 7. 18–end Ps. 119. 33–40 Luke 12. 54–end	Ps. 142; **144** Ecclus. 38. 1–14 or Ezek. 44. 4–16 John 16. 16–22	Ps. 145 2 Kings 24.18 – 25.12 1 Tim. 5. 1–16 *or First EP of Simon* *and Jude* Ps. 124; 125; 126 Deut. 32. 1–4 John 14. 15–26 **R ct**

28 Saturday   SIMON AND JUDE, APOSTLES

R		Isa. 28. 14–16 Ps. 119. 89–96 Eph. 2. 19–end John 15. 17–end	*MP*: Ps. 116; 117 Wisd. 5. 1–16 *or* Isa. 45. 18–end Luke 6. 12–16	*EP*: Ps. 119. 1–16 1 Macc. 2. 42–66 *or* Jer. 3. 11–18 Jude 1–4, 17–end

29 Sunday   THE LAST SUNDAY AFTER TRINITY   (Proper 25)*

G	*Track 1* Deut. 34. 1–12 Ps. 90. 1–6, 13–17 (or 90. 1–6) 1 Thess. 2. 1–8 Matt. 22. 34–end	*Track 2* Lev. 19. 1–2, 15–18 Ps. 1 1 Thess. 2. 1–8 Matt. 22. 34–end	Ps. 119. 137–152 Isa. 59. 9–20 Luke 14. 1–14	Ps. 119. 89–104 Eccles. chs 11 and 12 2 Tim. 2. 1–7 *Gospel*: Mark 12. 28–34
	or, if being observed as Bible Sunday:			
G		Neh. 8. 1–4a [5–6] 8–12 Ps. 119. 9–16 Col. 3. 12–17 Matt. 24. 30–35	Ps. 119. 137–152 Deut. 17. 14–15, 18–end John 5. 36b–end	Ps. 119. 89–104 Isa. 55. 1–11 Luke 4. 14–30

30 Monday

G **DEL 30**		Rom. 8. 12–17 Ps. 68. 1–6, 19 Luke 13. 10–17	Ps. **1**; 2; 3 Ecclus. 39. 1–11 *or* Eccles. ch. 1 John 17. 1–5	Ps. **4**; 7 Judith ch. 4 *or* Exod. 22. 21–27; 23. 1–17 1 Tim. 6. 1–10

31 Tuesday   *Martin Luther, Reformer, 1546*

G		Rom. 8. 18–25 Ps. 126 Luke 13. 18–21	Ps. **5**; 6; (8) Ecclus. 39. 13–end *or* Eccles. ch. 2 John 17. 6–19	*First EP of All Saints* Ps. 1; 5 Ecclus. 44. 1–15 *or* Isa. 40. 27–end Rev. 19. 6–10 **W ct** *or, if All Saints is* *observed on Sunday* *5 November*: Ps. **9**; 10† Judith 5.1 – 6.4 *or* Exod. 29.38 – 30.16 1 Tim. 6. 11–end

*If the Dedication Festival is kept on this Sunday, use the provision given on 30 September and 1 October.

Calendar and Holy Communion	Morning Prayer	Evening Prayer	NOTES

| G | | Ecclus. 38. 1–14
or Ezek. 44. 4–16
John 16. 16–22 | 2 Kings 24.18 – 25.12
1 Tim. 5. 1–16
or First EP of Simon
and Jude
(Ps. 124; 125; 126)
Deut. 32. 1–4
John 14. 15–26 | |

R ct

SIMON AND JUDE, APOSTLES

| R | Isa. 28. 9–16
Ps. 116. 11–end
Jude 1–8
or Rev. 21. 9–14
John 15. 17–end | (Ps. 119. 89–96)
Wisd. 5. 1–16
or Isa. 45. 18–end
Luke 6. 12–16 | (Ps. 119. 1–16)
1 Macc. 2. 42–66
or Jer. 3. 11–18
Eph. 2. 19–end | |

THE TWENTY-FIRST SUNDAY AFTER TRINITY

| G | Gen. 32. 24–29
Ps. 90. 1–12
Eph. 6. 10–20
John 4. 46b–end | Ps. 119. 137–152
Isa. 59. 9–20
Luke 14. 11–24 | Ps. 119. 89–104
Eccles. chs 11 and 12
2 Tim. 2. 1–7 | |

| G | | Ecclus. 39. 1–11
or Eccles. ch. 1
John 17. 1–5 | Judith ch. 4
or Exod. 22. 21–27;
23. 1–17
1 Tim. 6. 1–10 | |

| G | | Ecclus. 39. 13–end
or Eccles. ch. 2
John 17. 6–19 | First EP of All Saints
Ps. 1; 5
Ecclus. 44. 1–15
or Isa. 40. 27–end
Rev. 19. 6–10
𝖂 ct | |

	Sunday Principal Service Weekday Eucharist	Third Service Morning Prayer	Second Service Evening Prayer

November 2023

1 Wednesday **ALL SAINTS' DAY**

𝔴	Rev. 7. 9–end Ps. 34. 1–10 1 John 3. 1–3 Matt. 5. 1–12	MP: Ps. 15; 84; 149 Isa. ch. 35 Luke 9. 18–27	EP: Ps. 148; 150 Isa. 65. 17–end Heb. 11.32 – 12.2

or, if the readings above are used on Sunday 5 November:

𝔴	Isa. 56. 3–8 or 2 Esd. 2. 42–end Ps. 33. 1–5 Heb. 12. 18–24 Matt. 5. 1–12	MP: Ps. 111; 112; 117 Wisd. 5. 1–16 or Jer. 31. 31–34 2 Cor. 4. 5–12	EP: Ps. 145 Isa. 66. 20–23 Col. 1. 9–14

or, if kept as a feria:

G	Rom. 8. 26–30 Ps. 13 Luke 13. 22–30	Ps. 119. 1–32 Ecclus. 42. 15–end or Eccles. 3. 1–15 John 17. 20–end	Ps. 11; 12; 13 Judith 6.10 – 7.7 or Lev. ch. 8 2 Tim. 1. 1–14

2 Thursday   Commemoration of the Faithful Departed (All Souls' Day)

Rp or Gp	Lam. 3. 17–26, 31–33 or or Wisd. 3. 1–9 Ps. 23 or Ps. 27. 1–6, 16–end Rom. 5. 5–11 or 1 Pet. 1. 3–9 John 5. 19–25 or John 6. 37–40	Rom. 8. 31–end Ps. 109. 20–26, 29–30 Luke 13. 31–end	Ps. 14; 15; 16 Ecclus. 43. 1–12 or Eccles. 3.16 – 4.end John 18. 1–11	Ps. 18† Judith 7. 19–end or Lev. ch. 9 2 Tim. 1.15 – 2.13

3 Friday   Richard Hooker, Priest, Anglican Apologist, Teacher, 1600
Martin of Porres, Friar, 1639

Rw or Gw	Com. Teacher or esp. John 16. 12–15 also Ecclus. 44. 10–15	Rom. 9. 1–5 Ps. 147. 13–end Luke 14. 1–6	Ps. 17; 19 Ecclus. 43. 13–end or Eccles. ch. 5 John 18. 12–27	Ps. 22 Judith 8. 9–end or Lev. 16. 2–24 2 Tim. 2. 14–end

4 Saturday

R or G	Rom. 11. 1–2, 11–12, 25–29 Ps. 94. 14–19 Luke 14. 1, 7–11	Ps. 20; 21; 23 Ecclus. 44. 1–15 or Eccles. ch. 6 John 18. 28–end	Ps. 24; 25 Judith ch. 9 or Lev. ch. 17 2 Tim. ch. 3 ct

5 Sunday   THE FOURTH SUNDAY BEFORE ADVENT

R or G	Mic. 3. 5–end Ps. 43 or Ps. 107. 1–8 1 Thess. 2. 9–13 Matt. 24. 1–14	Ps. 33 Isa. 66. 20–23 Eph. 1. 11–end	Ps. 111; 117 Dan. 7. 1–18 Luke 6. 17–31

Or ALL SAINTS' SUNDAY (see readings for 1 November throughout the day)

𝔴

6 Monday   *Leonard, Hermit, 6th century; William Temple, Archbishop of Canterbury, Teacher, 1944*

R or G DEL 31	Rom. 11. 29–end Ps. 69. 31–37 Luke 14. 12–14	Ps. 2; 146 alt. Ps. 27; 30 Isa. 1. 1–20 Matt. 1. 18–end	Ps. 92; 96; 97 alt. Ps. 26; 28; 29 Dan. ch. 1 Rev. ch. 1

Calendar and Holy Communion	Morning Prayer	Evening Prayer	NOTES

ALL SAINTS' DAY

w Isa. 66. 20–23
Ps. 33. 1–5
Rev. 7. 2–4 [5–8] 9–12
Matt. 5. 1–12

Ps. 15; 84; 149
Isa. ch. 35
Luke 9. 18–27

Ps. 148; 150
Isa. 65. 17–end
Heb. 11.32 – 12.2

To celebrate All Souls' Day, see *Common Worship* provision.

G

Ecclus. 43. 1–12
or Eccles. 3.16 – 4.end
John 18. 1–11

Judith 7. 19–end
or Lev. ch. 9
2 Tim. 1.15 – 2.13

G

Ecclus. 43. 13–end
or Eccles. ch. 5
John 18. 12–27

Judith 8. 9–end
or Lev. 16. 2–24
2 Tim. 2. 14–end

G

Ecclus. 44. 1–15
or Eccles. ch. 6
John 18. 28–end

Judith ch. 9
or Lev. ch. 17
2 Tim. ch. 3

ct

THE TWENTY-SECOND SUNDAY AFTER TRINITY

G Gen. 45. 1–7, 15
Ps. 133
Phil. 1. 3–11
Matt. 18. 21–end

Ps. 33
Isa. 66. 20–23
Eph. 1. 11–end

Ps. 111; 117
Dan. 7. 1–18
Luke 6. 17–31

Leonard, Hermit, 6th century

Gw Com. Abbot

Isa. 1. 1–20
Matt. 1. 18–end

Dan. ch. 1
Rev. ch. 1

	Sunday Principal Service / Weekday Eucharist	Third Service / Morning Prayer	Second Service / Evening Prayer
7 Tuesday	**Willibrord of York, Bishop, Apostle of Frisia, 739**		
Rw *or* **Gw**	Com. Missionary *or* Rom. 12. 5–16 *esp.* Isa. 52. 7–10 Ps. 131 Matt. 28. 16–end Luke 14. 15–24	Ps. **5**; 147. 1–12 *alt.* Ps. 32; **36** Isa. 1. 21–end Matt. 2. 1–15	Ps. 98; 99; **100** *alt.* Ps. 33 Dan. 2. 1–24 Rev. 2. 1–11
8 Wednesday	**The Saints and Martyrs of England**		
Rw *or* **Gw**	Isa. 61. 4–9 *or* Ecclus. 44. 1–15 Ps. 15 Rev. 19. 5–10 John 17. 18–23 Rom. 13. 8–10 Ps. 112 Luke 14. 25–33	Ps. **9**; 147. 13–end *alt.* Ps. 34 Isa. 2. 1–11 Matt. 2. 16–end	Ps. 111; **112**; 116 *alt.* Ps. 119. 33–56 Dan. 2. 25–end Rev. 2. 12–end
9 Thursday	*Margery Kempe, Mystic, c. 1440*		
R *or* **G**	Rom. 14. 7–12 Ps. 27. 14–end Luke 15. 1–10	Ps. 11; **15**; 148 *alt.* Ps. 37† Isa. 2. 12–end Matt. ch. 3	Ps. 118 *alt.* Ps. 39; **40** Dan. 3. 1–18 Rev. 3. 1–13
10 Friday	**Leo the Great, Bishop of Rome, Teacher, 461**		
Rw *or* **Gw**	Com. Teacher *or* Rom. 15. 14–21 *also* 1 Pet. 5. 1–11 Ps. 98 Luke 16. 1–8	Ps. **16**; 149 *alt.* Ps. 31 Isa. 3. 1–15 Matt. 4. 1–11	Ps. 137; 138; **143** *alt.* Ps. 35 Dan. 3. 19–end Rev. 3. 14–end
11 Saturday	**Martin, Bishop of Tours, c. 397**		
Rw *or* **Gw**	Com. Bishop *or* Rom. 16. 3–9, 16, *also* 1 Thess. 5. 1–11 22–end Matt. 25. 34–40 Ps. 145. 1–7 Luke 16. 9–15	Ps. **18. 31–end**; 150 *alt.* Ps. 41; **42**; 43 Isa. 4.2 – 5.7 Matt. 4. 12–22	Ps. 145 *alt.* Ps. 45; **46** Dan. 4. 1–18 Rev. ch. 4 **ct**
12 Sunday	**THE THIRD SUNDAY BEFORE ADVENT** (Remembrance Sunday)		
R *or* **G**	Wisd. 6. 12–16 *or* *Canticle:* Wisd. 6. 17–20 1 Thess. 4. 13–end Matt. 25. 1–13 Amos 5. 18–24 Ps. 70 1 Thess. 4. 13–end Matt. 25. 1–13	Ps. 91 Deut. 17. 14–end 1 Tim. 2. 1–7	Ps. [20]; 82 Judg. 7. 2–22 John 15. 9–17
13 Monday	**Charles Simeon, Priest, Evangelical Divine, 1836**		
Rw *or* **Gw** **DEL 32**	Com. Pastor *or* Wisd. 1. 1–7 *esp.* Mal. 2. 5–7 *or* Titus 1. 1–9 *also* Col. 1. 3–8 Ps. 139. 1–9 Luke 8. 4–8 *or* Ps. 24. 1–6 Luke 17. 1–6	Ps. 19; **20** *alt.* Ps. 44 Isa. 5. 8–24 Matt. 4.23 – 5.12	Ps. 34 *alt.* Ps. **47**; 49 Dan. 4. 19–end Rev. ch. 5
14 Tuesday	*Samuel Seabury, first Anglican Bishop in North America, 1796*		
R *or* **G**	Wisd. 2.23 – 3.9 *or* Titus 2. 1–8, 11–14 Ps. 34. 1–6 *or* Ps. 37. 3–5, 30–32 Luke 17. 7–10	Ps. **21**; 24 *alt.* Ps. **48**; 52 Isa. 5. 25–end Matt. 5. 13–20	Ps. 36; **40** *alt.* Ps. 50 Dan. 5. 1–12 Rev. ch. 6
15 Wednesday			
R *or* **G**	Wisd. 6. 1–11 *or* Titus 3. 1–7 Ps. 82 *or* Ps. 23 Luke 17. 11–19	Ps. **23**; 25 *alt.* Ps. 119. 57–80 Isa. ch. 6 Matt. 5. 21–37	Ps. 37 *alt.* Ps. **59**; 60; (67) Dan. 5. 13–end Rev. 7. 1–4, 9–end

Calendar and Holy Communion		Morning Prayer	Evening Prayer	NOTES
G		Isa. 1. 21–end Matt. 2. 1–15	Dan. 2. 1–24 Rev. 2. 1–11	
G		Isa. 2. 1–11 Matt. 2. 16–end	Dan. 2. 25–end Rev. 2. 12–end	
G		Isa. 2. 12–end Matt. ch. 3	Dan. 3. 1–18 Rev. 3. 1–13	
G		Isa. 3. 1–15 Matt. 4. 1–11	Dan. 3. 19–end Rev. 3. 14–end	
Martin, Bishop of Tours, c. 397				
Gw	Com. Bishop	Isa. 4.2 – 5.7 Matt. 4. 12–22	Dan. 4. 1–18 Rev. ch. 4	
			ct	
THE TWENTY-THIRD SUNDAY AFTER TRINITY				
G	Isa. 11. 1–10 Ps. 44. 1–9 Phil. 3. 17–end Matt. 22. 15–22	Ps. 91 Deut. 17. 14–end 1 Tim. 2. 1–7	Ps. [20]; 82 Judg. 7. 2–22 John 15. 9–17	
Britius, Bishop of Tours, 444				
Gw	Com. Bishop	Isa. 5. 8–24 Matt. 4.23 – 5.12	Dan. 4. 19–end Rev. ch. 5	
G		Isa. 5. 25–end Matt. 5. 13–20	Dan. 5. 1–12 Rev. ch. 6	
Machutus, Bishop, Apostle of Brittany, c. 564				
Gw	Com. Bishop	Isa. ch. 6 Matt. 5. 21–37	Dan. 5. 13–end Rev. 7. 1–4, 9–end	

		Sunday Principal Service	Third Service	Second Service
		Weekday Eucharist	Morning Prayer	Evening Prayer

16 Thursday   **Margaret, Queen of Scotland, Philanthropist, Reformer of the Church, 1093**
Edmund Rich of Abingdon, Archbishop of Canterbury, 1240

Rw *or* **Gw**	Com. Saint *or*	Wisd. 7.22 – 8.1	Ps. *26*; 27	Ps. 42; *43*
	also Prov. 31. 10–12,	*or* Philem. 7–20	*alt.* Ps. 56; *57*; (63†)	*alt.* Ps. 61; *62*; 64
	20, 26–end	Ps. 119. 89–96	Isa. 7. 1–17	Dan. ch. 6
	1 Cor. 12.13 – 13.3	*or* Ps. 146. 4–end	Matt. 5. 38–end	Rev. ch. 8
	Matt. 25. 34–end	Luke 17. 20–25		

17 Friday   **Hugh, Bishop of Lincoln, 1200**

Rw *or* **Gw**	Com. Bishop *or*	Wisd. 13. 1–9	Ps. 28; *32*	Ps. 31
	also 1 Tim. 6. 11–16	*or* 2 John 4–9	*alt.* Ps. *51*; 54	*alt.* Ps. 38
		Ps. 19. 1–4	Isa. 8. 1–15	Dan. 7. 1–14
		or Ps. 119. 1–8	Matt. 6. 1–18	Rev. 9. 1–12
		Luke 17. 26–end		

18 Saturday   **Elizabeth of Hungary, Princess of Thuringia, Philanthropist, 1231**

Rw *or* **Gw**	Com. Saint *or*	Wisd. 18. 14–16;	Ps. 33	Ps. 84; *86*
	esp. Matt. 25. 31–end	19. 6–9	*alt.* Ps. 68	*alt.* Ps. 65; *66*
	also Prov. 31. 10–end	*or* 3 John 5–8	Isa. 8.16 – 9.7	Dan. 7. 15–end
		Ps. 105. 1–5, 35–42	Matt. 6. 19–end	Rev. 9. 13–end
		or Ps. 112		
		Luke 18. 1–8		**ct**

19 Sunday   **THE SECOND SUNDAY BEFORE ADVENT**

R *or* **G**		Zeph. 1. 7, 12–end	Ps. 98	Ps. 89. 19–37
		Ps. 90. 1–8 [9–11] 12	Dan. 10. 19–end	(*or* 89. 19–29)
		(*or* 90. 1–8)	Rev. ch. 4	1 Kings 1. [1–14] 15–40
		1 Thess. 5. 1–11		Rev. 1. 4–18
		Matt. 25. 14–30		*Gospel:* Luke 9. 1–6

20 Monday   **Edmund, King of the East Angles, Martyr, 870**
Priscilla Lydia Sellon, a Restorer of the Religious Life in the Church of England, 1876

R *or* **Gr**	Com. Martyr *or*	1 Macc. 1. 10–15,	Ps. 46; *47*	Ps. 70; *71*
DEL 33	*also* Prov. 20. 28;	41–43, 54–57, 62–64	*alt.* Ps. 71	*alt.* Ps. *72*; 75
	21. 1–4, 7	*or* Rev. 1. 1–4; 2. 1–5	Isa. 9.8 – 10.4	Dan. 8. 1–14
		Ps. 79. 1–5	Matt. 7. 1–12	Rev. ch. 10
		or Ps. 1		
		Luke 18. 35–end		

21 Tuesday

R *or* **G**		2 Macc. 6. 18–end	Ps. 48; *52*	Ps. *67*; 72
		or Rev. 3. 1–6, 14–31	*alt.* Ps. 73	*alt.* Ps. 74
		Ps. 11	Isa. 10. 5–19	Dan. 8. 15–end
		or Ps. 15	Matt. 7. 13–end	Rev. 11. 1–14
		Luke 19. 1–10		

22 Wednesday   *Cecilia, Martyr at Rome, c. 230*

R *or* **G**		2 Macc. 7. 1, 20–31	Ps. *56*; 57	Ps. 73
		or Rev. ch. 4	*alt.* Ps. 77	*alt.* Ps. 119. 81–104
		Ps. 116. 10–end	Isa. 10. 20–32	Dan. 9. 1–19
		or Ps. 150	Matt. 8. 1–13	Rev. 11. 15–end
		Luke 19. 11–28		

23 Thursday   **Clement, Bishop of Rome, Martyr, c. 100**

R *or* **Gr**	Com. Martyr *or*	1 Macc. 2. 15–29	Ps. 61; *62*	Ps. 74; *76*
	also Phil. 3.17 – 4.3	*or* Rev. 5. 1–10	*alt.* Ps. 78. 1–39†	*alt.* Ps. 78. 40–end†
	Matt. 16. 13–19	Ps. 129	Isa. 10.33 – 11.9	Dan. 9. 20–end
		or Ps. 149. 1–5	Matt. 8. 14–22	Rev. ch. 12
		Luke 19. 41–44		

Calendar and Holy Communion	Morning Prayer	Evening Prayer	NOTES
G	Isa. 7. 1–17 Matt. 5. 38–end	Dan. ch. 6 Rev. ch. 8	
Hugh, Bishop of Lincoln, 1200			
Gw Com. Bishop	Isa. 8. 1–15 Matt. 6. 1–18	Dan. 7. 1–14 Rev. 9. 1–12	
G	Isa. 8.16 – 9.7 Matt. 6. 19–end	Dan. 7. 15–end Rev. 9. 13–end	
		ct	
THE TWENTY-FOURTH SUNDAY AFTER TRINITY			
G Isa. 55. 6–11 Ps. 85. 1–7 Col. 1. 3–12 Matt. 9. 18–26	Ps. 98 Dan. 10. 19–end Rev. ch. 4	Ps. 89. 19–37 (or 89. 19–29) 1 Kings 1. [1–14] 15–40 Rev. 1. 4–18	
Edmund, King of the East Angles, Martyr, 870			
Gr Com. Martyr	Isa. 9.8 – 10.4 Matt. 7. 1–12	Dan. 8. 1–14 Rev. ch. 10	
G	Isa. 10. 5–19 Matt. 7. 13–end	Dan. 8. 15–end Rev. 11. 1–14	
Cecilia, Martyr at Rome, c. 230			
Gr Com. Virgin Martyr	Isa. 10. 20–32 Matt. 8. 1–13	Dan. 9. 1–19 Rev. 11. 15–end	
Clement, Bishop of Rome, Martyr, c. 100			
Gr Com. Martyr	Isa. 10.33 – 11.9 Matt. 8. 14–22	Dan. 9. 20–end Rev. ch. 12	

		Sunday Principal Service Weekday Eucharist	Third Service Morning Prayer	Second Service Evening Prayer

24 Friday

R or G		1 Macc. 4. 36–37, 52–59 or Rev. 10. 8–11 Ps. 122 or Ps. 119. 65–72 Luke 19. 45–48	Ps. *63*; 65 *alt.* Ps. 55 Isa. 11.10 – 12.end Matt. 8. 23–end	Ps. 77 *alt.* Ps. 69 Dan. 10.1 – 11.1 Rev. 13. 1–10

25 Saturday   *Catherine of Alexandria, Martyr, 4th century; Isaac Watts, Hymn Writer, 1748*

R or G		1 Macc. 6. 1–13 or Rev. 11. 4–12 Ps. 124 or Ps. 144. 1–9 Luke 20. 27–40	Ps. 78. 1–39 *alt.* Ps. *76*; 79 Isa. 13. 1–13 Matt. 9. 1–17	Ps. 78. 40–end *alt.* Ps. 81; *84* Dan. ch. 12 Rev. 13. 11–end **ct** *or First EP of Christ the King* Ps. 99; 100 Isa. 10.33 – 11.9 1 Tim. 6. 11–16 **R** *or* **W ct**

26 Sunday   **CHRIST THE KING**
The Sunday Next Before Advent

R or W		Ezek. 34. 11–16, 20–24 Ps. 95. 1–7 Eph. 1. 15–end Matt. 25. 31–end	*MP*: Ps. 29; 110 Isa. 4.2 – 5.7 Luke 19. 29–38	*EP*: Ps. 93; [97] 2 Sam. 23. 1–7 *or* 1 Macc. 2. 15–29 Matt. 28. 16–end

27 Monday

R *or* G **DEL 34**		Dan. 1. 1–6, 8–20 *Canticle*: Bless the Lord Luke 21. 1–4	Ps. 92; *96* *alt.* Ps. *80*; 82 Isa. 14. 3–20 Matt. 9. 18–34	Ps. *80*; 81 *alt.* Ps. *85*; 86 Isa. 40. 1–11 Rev. 14. 1–13

28 Tuesday

R *or* G		Dan. 2. 31–45 *Canticle*: Benedicite 1–3 Luke 21. 5–11	Ps. *97*; 98; 100 *alt.* Ps. 87; *89. 1–18* Isa. ch. 17 Matt. 9.35 – 10.15	Ps. 99; *101* *alt.* Ps. 89. 19–end Isa. 40. 12–26 Rev. 14.14 – 15.end

29 Wednesday

R *or* G		Dan. 5. 1–6, 13–14, 16–17, 23–28 *Canticle*: Benedicite 4–5 Luke 21. 12–19	Ps. 110; 111; *112* *alt.* Ps. 119. 105–128 Isa. ch. 19 Matt. 10. 16–33	Ps. 121; *122*; 123; 124 *alt.* Ps. *91*; 93 Isa. 40.27 – 41.7 Rev. 16. 1–11 *or First EP of Andrew the Apostle* Ps. 48 Isa. 49. 1–9a 1 Cor. 4. 9–16 **R ct**

Day of Intercession and Thanksgiving for the Missionary Work of the Church:

R *or* G		Isa. 49. 1–6; Isa. 52. 7–10; Mic. 4. 1–5 Ps. 2; 46; 47 Acts 17. 12–end; 2 Cor. 5.14 – 6.2; Eph. 2. 13–end Matt. 5. 13–16; Matt. 28. 16–end; John 17. 20–end		

Calendar and Holy Communion	Morning Prayer	Evening Prayer	NOTES
G	Isa. 11.10 – 12.end Matt. 8. 23–end	Dan. 10.1 – 11.1 Rev. 13. 1–10	

Catherine of Alexandria, Martyr, 4th century

Gr Com. Virgin Martyr	Isa. 13. 1–13 Matt. 9. 1–17	Dan. ch. 12 Rev. 13. 11–end	
		ct	

THE SUNDAY NEXT BEFORE ADVENT
To celebrate Christ the King, see *Common Worship* provision.

G Jer. 23. 5–8 Ps. 85. 8–end Col. 1. 13–20 John 6. 5–14	Ps. 29; 110 Isa. 4.2 – 5.7 Luke 19. 29–38	Ps. 93; [97] 2 Sam. 23. 1–7 *or* 1 Macc. 2. 15–29 Matt. 28. 16–end	
G	Isa. 14. 3–20 Matt. 9. 18–34	Isa. 40. 1–11 Rev. 14. 1–13	
G	Isa. ch. 17 Matt. 9.35 – 10.15	Isa. 40. 12–26 Rev. 14.14 – 15.end	
G	Isa. ch. 19 Matt. 10. 16–33	Isa. 40.27 – 41.7 Rev. 16. 1–11 *or First EP of Andrew the Apostle* (Ps. 48) Isa. 49. 1–9a 1 Cor. 4. 9–16	
		R ct	

To celebrate the Day of Intercession and Thanksgiving for the Missionary Work of the Church, see *Common Worship* provision.

		Sunday Principal Service Weekday Eucharist	Third Service Morning Prayer	Second Service Evening Prayer

30 Thursday   **ANDREW THE APOSTLE**

R		Isa. 52. 7–10 Ps. 19. 1–6 Rom. 10. 12–18 Matt. 4. 18–22	*MP*: Ps. 47; 147. 1–12 Ezek. 47. 1–12 *or* Ecclus. 14. 20–end John 12. 20–32	*EP*: Ps. 87; 96 Zech. 8. 20–end John 1. 35–42

December 2023

1 Friday   *Charles de Foucauld, Hermit in the Sahara, 1916*

R *or* G		Dan. 7. 2–14 *Canticle*: Benedicite 8b–10a Luke 21. 29–33	Ps. 139 *alt*. Ps. **88**; (95) Isa. 22. 1–14 Matt. 11. 2–19	Ps. **146**; 147 *alt*. Ps. 102 Isa. 41.21 – 42.9 Rev. ch. 17

2 Saturday

R *or* G		Dan. 7. 15–27 *Canticle*: Benedicite 10b–end Luke 21. 34–36	Ps. 145 *alt*. Ps. 96; **97**; 100 Isa. ch. 24 Matt. 11. 20–end	Ps. 148; 149; **150** *alt*. Ps. 104 Isa. 42. 10–17 Rev. ch. 18 **P** ct

3 Sunday   **THE FIRST SUNDAY OF ADVENT**
Common Worship Year B begins

P		Isa. 64. 1–9 Ps. 80. 1–8, 18–20 (*or* 80. 1–8) 1 Cor. 1. 3–9 Mark 13. 24–end	Ps. 44 Isa. 2. 1–5 Luke 12. 35–48	Ps. 25 (*or* 25. 1–9) Isa. 1. 1–20 Matt. 21. 1–13

4 Monday   *John of Damascus, Monk, Teacher, c. 749; Nicholas Ferrar, Deacon, Founder of the Little Gidding Community, 163*
Daily Eucharistic Lectionary Year 2 begins

P		Isa. 2. 1–5 Ps. 122 Matt. 8. 5–11	Ps. **50**; 54 *alt*. Ps. **1**; 2; 3 Isa. 25. 1–9 Matt. 12. 1–21	Ps. 70; **71** *alt*. Ps. **4**; 7 Isa. 42. 18–end Rev. ch. 19

5 Tuesday

P		Isa. 11. 1–10 Ps. 72. 1–4, 18–19 Luke 10. 21–24	Ps. **80**; 82 *alt*. Ps. **5**; 6; (8) Isa. 26. 1–13 Matt. 12. 22–37	Ps. **74**; 75 *alt*. Ps. **9**; 10† Isa. 43. 1–13 Rev. ch. 20

6 Wednesday   **Nicholas, Bishop of Myra, *c.* 326**

Pw		Com. Bishop *or* Isa. 25. 6–10a *also* Isa. 61. 1–3 Ps. 23 1 Tim. 6. 6–11 Matt. 15. 29–37 Mark 10. 13–16	Ps. 5; **7** *alt*. Ps. 119. 1–32 Isa. 28. 1–13 Matt. 12. 38–end	Ps. 76; **77** *alt*. Ps. **11**; 12; 13 Isa. 43. 14–end Rev. 21. 1–8

7 Thursday   **Ambrose, Bishop of Milan, Teacher, 397**

Pw		Com. Teacher *or* Isa. 26. 1–6 *also* Isa. 41. 9b–13 Ps. 118. 18–27a Luke 22. 24–30 Matt. 7. 21, 24–27	Ps. **42**; 43 *alt*. Ps. 14; **15**; 16 Isa. 28. 14–end Matt. 13. 1–23	Ps. **40**; 46 *alt*. Ps. 18† Isa. 44. 1–8 Rev. 21. 9–21

8 Friday   **The Conception of the Blessed Virgin Mary**

Pw		Com. BVM *or* Isa. 29. 17–end Ps. 27. 1–4, 16–17 Matt. 9. 27–31	Ps. **25**; 26 *alt*. Ps. 17; **19** Isa. 29. 1–14 Matt. 13. 24–43	Ps. 16; **17** *alt*. Ps. 22 Isa. 44. 9–23 Rev. 21.22 – 22.5

Calendar and Holy Communion	Morning Prayer	Evening Prayer	NOTES
ANDREW THE APOSTLE			
R Zech. 8. 20–end Ps. 92. 1–5 Rom. 10. 9–end Matt. 4. 18–22	(Ps. 47; 147. 1–12) Ezek. 47. 1–12 or Ecclus. 14. 20–end John 12. 20–32	(Ps. 87; 96) Isa. 52. 7–10 John 1. 35–42	
G	Isa. 22. 1–14 Matt. 11. 2–19	Isa. 41.21 – 42.9 Rev. ch. 17	
G	Isa. ch. 24 Matt. 11. 20–end	Isa. 42. 10–17 Rev. ch. 18	
		P ct	
THE FIRST SUNDAY IN ADVENT Advent 1 Collect until Christmas Eve			
P Mic. 4. 1–4, 6–7 Ps. 25. 1–9 Rom. 13. 8–14 Matt. 21. 1–13	Ps. 44 Isa. 2. 1–5 Luke 12. 35–48	Ps. 9 Isa. 1. 1–20 Mark 13. 24–end	
P	Isa. 25. 1–9 Matt. 12. 1–21	Isa. 42. 18–end Rev. ch. 19	
P	Isa. 26. 1–13 Matt. 12. 22–37	Isa. 43. 1–13 Rev. ch. 20	
Nicholas, Bishop of Myra, c. 326			
Pw Com. Bishop	Isa. 28. 1–13 Matt. 12. 38–end	Isa. 43. 14–end Rev. 21. 1–8	
P	Isa. 28. 14–end Matt. 13. 1–23	Isa. 44. 1–8 Rev. 21. 9–21	
The Conception of the Blessed Virgin Mary			
Pw	Isa. 29. 1–14 Matt. 13. 24–43	Isa. 44. 9–23 Rev. 21.22 – 22.5	

	Sunday Principal Service Weekday Eucharist	Third Service Morning Prayer	Second Service Evening Prayer
9 Saturday			
P	Isa. 30. 19–21, 23–26 Ps. 146. 4–9 Matt. 9.35 – 10.1, 6–8	Ps. **9**; (10) *alt.* Ps. 20; 21; **23** Isa. 29. 15–end Matt. 13. 44–end	Ps. **27**; 28 *alt.* Ps. **24**; 25 Isa. 44.24 – 45.13 Rev. 22. 6–end **ct**
10 Sunday	THE SECOND SUNDAY OF ADVENT		
P	Isa. 40. 1–11 Ps. 85. 1–2, 8–end (*or* 85. 8–end) 2 Pet. 3. 8–15a Mark 1. 1–8	Ps. 80 Baruch 5. 1–9 *or* Zeph. 3. 14–end Luke 1. 5–20	Ps. 40 (*or* 40. 12–end) 1 Kings 22. 1–28 Rom. 15. 4–13 *Gospel:* Matt. 11. 2–11
11 Monday			
P	Isa. ch. 35 Ps. 85. 7–end Luke 5. 17–26	Ps. 44 *alt.* Ps. 27; **30** Isa. 30. 1–18 Matt. 14. 1–12	Ps. **144**; 146 *alt.* Ps. 26; **28**; 29 Isa. 45. 14–end 1 Thess. ch. 1
12 Tuesday			
P	Isa. 40. 1–11 Ps. 96. 1, 10–end Matt. 18. 12–14	Ps. **56**; 57 *alt.* Ps. 32; **36** Isa. 30. 19–end Matt. 14. 13–end	Ps. **11**; 12; 13 *alt.* Ps. 33 Isa. ch. 46 1 Thess. 2. 1–12
13 Wednesday	Lucy, Martyr at Syracuse, 304 Ember Day* *Samuel Johnson, Moralist, 1784*		
Pr	Com. Martyr *or* Isa. 40. 25–end *also* Wisd. 3. 1–7 Ps. 103. 8–13 2 Cor. 4. 6–15 Matt. 11. 28–end	Ps. **62**; 63 *alt.* Ps. 34 Isa. ch. 31 Matt. 15. 1–20	Ps. **10**; 14 *alt.* Ps. 119. 33–56 Isa. ch. 47 1 Thess. 2. 13–end
14 Thursday	John of the Cross, Poet, Teacher, 1591		
Pw	Com. Teacher *or* Isa. 41. 13–20 *esp.* 1 Cor. 2. 1–10 Ps. 145. 1, 8–13 *also* John 14. 18–23 Matt. 11. 11–15	Ps. 53; **54**; 60 *alt.* Ps. 37† Isa. ch. 32 Matt. 15. 21–28	Ps. 73 *alt.* Ps. 39; **40** Isa. 48. 1–11 1 Thess. ch. 3
15 Friday	Ember Day*		
P	Isa. 48. 17–19 Ps. 1 Matt. 11. 16–19	Ps. 85; **86** *alt.* Ps. 31 Isa. 33. 1–22 Matt. 15. 29–end	Ps. 82; **90** *alt.* Ps. 35 Isa. 48. 12–end 1 Thess. 4. 1–12
16 Saturday	Ember Day*		
P	Ecclus. 48. 1–4, 9–11 *or* 2 Kings 2. 9–12 Ps. 80. 1–4, 18–19 Matt. 17. 10–13	Ps. 145 *alt.* Ps. 41; **42**; 43 Isa. ch. 35 Matt. 16. 1–12	Ps. 93; **94** *alt.* Ps. 45; **46** Isa. 49. 1–13 1 Thess. 4. 13–end **ct**

*For Ember Day provision, see p. 11.

	Calendar and Holy Communion	Morning Prayer	Evening Prayer	NOTES
P		Isa. 29. 15–end Matt. 13. 44–end	Isa. 44.24 – 45.13 Rev. 22. 6–end	
			ct	
	THE SECOND SUNDAY IN ADVENT			
P	2 Kings 22. 8–10; 23. 1–3 Ps. 50. 1–6 Rom. 15. 4–13 Luke 21. 25–33	Ps. 80 Baruch 5. 1–9 or Zeph. 3. 14–end Luke 1. 5–20	Ps. 40 (or 40. 12–end) 1 Kings 22. 1–28 2 Pet. 3. 8–15a	
P		Isa. 30. 1–18 Matt. 14. 1–12	Isa. 45. 14–end 1 Thess. ch. 1	
P		Isa. 30. 19–end Matt. 14. 13–end	Isa. ch. 46 1 Thess. 2. 1–12	
	Lucy, Martyr at Syracuse, 304 Ember Day			
Pr	Com. Virgin Martyr or Ember CEG	Isa. ch. 31 Matt. 15. 1–20	Isa. ch. 47 1 Thess. 2. 13–end	
P		Isa. ch. 32 Matt. 15. 21–28	Isa. 48. 1–11 1 Thess. ch. 3	
	Ember Day			
P	Ember CEG	Isa. 33. 1–22 Matt. 15. 29–end	Isa. 48. 12–end 1 Thess. 4. 1–12	
	O Sapientia Ember Day			
P	Ember CEG	Isa. ch. 35 Matt. 16. 1–12	Isa. 49. 1–13 1 Thess. 4. 13–end	
			ct	

	Sunday Principal Service Weekday Eucharist	Third Service Morning Prayer	Second Service Evening Prayer
17 Sunday THE THIRD SUNDAY OF ADVENT O Sapientia*			
P	Isa. 61. 1–4, 8–end Ps. 126 *or Canticle:* Magnificat 1 Thess. 5. 16–24 John 1. 6–8, 19–28	Ps. 50. 1–6; 62 Isa. ch. 12 Luke 1. 57–66	Ps. 68. 1–19 (or 68. 1–8) Mal. 3. 1–4; ch. 4 Phil. 4. 4–7 *Gospel:* Matt. 14. 1–12
18 Monday			
P	Jer. 23. 5–8 Ps. 72. 1–2, 12–13, 18–end Matt. 1. 18–24	Ps. 40 *alt.* Ps. 44 Isa. 38. 1–8, 21–22 Matt. 16. 13–end	Ps. 25; *26* *alt.* Ps. *47*; 49 Isa. 49. 14–25 1 Thess. 5. 1–11
19 Tuesday			
P	Judg. 13. 2–7, 24–end Ps. 71. 3–8 Luke 1. 5–25	Ps. 144; *146* Isa. 38. 9–20 Matt. 17. 1–13	Ps. 10; *57* Isa. ch. 50 1 Thess. 5. 12–end
20 Wednesday			
P	Isa. 7. 10–14 Ps. 24. 1–6 Luke 1. 26–38	Ps. *46*; 95 Isa. ch. 39 Matt. 17. 14–21	Ps. *4*; 9 Isa. 51. 1–8 2 Thess. ch. 1
21 Thursday**			
P	Zeph. 3. 14–18 Ps. 33. 1–4, 11–12, 20–end Luke 1. 39–45	Ps. *121*; 122; 123 Zeph. 1.1 – 2.3 Matt. 17. 22–end	Ps. 80; *84* Isa. 51. 9–16 2 Thess. ch. 2
22 Friday			
P	1 Sam. 1. 24–end Ps. 113 Luke 1. 46–56	Ps. *124*; 125; 126; 127 Zeph. 3. 1–13 Matt. 18. 1–20	Ps. 24; *48* Isa. 51. 17–end 2 Thess. ch. 3
23 Saturday			
P	Mal. 3. 1–4; 4. 5–end Ps. 25. 3–9 Luke 1. 57–66	Ps. 128; 129; *130*; 131 Zeph. 3. 14–end Matt. 18. 21–end	Ps. 89. 1–37 Isa. 52. 1–12 Jude ct
24 Sunday THE FOURTH SUNDAY OF ADVENT CHRISTMAS EVE			
P	2 Sam. 7. 1–11, 16 *Canticle:* Magnificat *or* Ps. 89. 1–4, 19–26 (*or* 1–8) Rom. 16. 25–end Luke 1. 26–38	Ps. 144 Isa. 7. 10–16 Rom. 1. 1–7	*Evening Prayer* Ps. 85 Zech. ch. 2 Rev. 1. 1–8

*Evening Prayer readings from the Additional Weekday Lectionary (see p. 119) may be used from 17 to 23 December.
**Thomas the Apostle may be celebrated on 21 December instead of 3 July.

Calendar and Holy Communion	Morning Prayer	Evening Prayer	NOTES

THE THIRD SUNDAY IN ADVENT

P Isa. ch. 35 Ps. 80. 1–7 1 Cor. 4. 1–5 Matt. 11. 2–10	Ps. 62 Isa. ch. 12 Luke 1. 57–66	Ps. 68. 1–19 (or 68. 1–8) Mal. 3. 1–4; ch. 4 Matt. 14. 1–12	
P	Isa. 38. 1–8, 21–22 Matt. 16. 13–end	Isa. 49. 14–25 1 Thess. 5. 1–11	
P	Isa. 38. 9–20 Matt. 17. 1–13	Isa. ch. 50 1 Thess. 5. 12–end	
P	Isa. ch. 39 Matt. 17. 14–21	Isa. 51. 1–8 2 Thess. ch. 1 or First EP of Thomas the Apostle (Ps. 27) Isa. ch. 35 Heb. 10.35 – 11.1 **R ct**	

THOMAS THE APOSTLE

R Job 42. 1–6 Ps. 139. 1–11 Eph. 2. 19–end John 20. 24–end	(Ps. 92; 146) 2 Sam. 15. 17–21 or Ecclus. ch. 2 John 11. 1–16	(Ps. 139) Hab. 2. 1–4 1 Pet. 1. 3–12	
P	Zeph. 3. 1–13 Matt. 18. 1–20	Isa. 51. 17–end 2 Thess. ch. 3	
P	Zeph. 3. 14–end Matt. 18. 21–end	Isa. 52. 1–12 Jude **ct**	

THE FOURTH SUNDAY IN ADVENT
CHRISTMAS EVE

P Collect (1) Christmas Eve (2) Advent 1 Isa. 40. 1–9 Ps. 145. 17–end Phil. 4. 4–7 John 1. 19–28	Ps. 144 Isa. 7. 10–16 Rom. 1. 1–7	Ps. 85 Zech. ch. 2 Rev. 1. 1–8	

	Sunday Principal Service Weekday Eucharist	Third Service Morning Prayer	Second Service Evening Prayer
25 Monday	**CHRISTMAS DAY**		
𝖜	*Any of the following sets of readings may be used on the evening of Christmas Eve and on Christmas Day. Set III should be used at some service during the celebration.*	*I* Isa. 9. 2–7 Ps. 96 Titus 2. 11–14 Luke 2. 1–14 [15–20] *II* Isa. 62. 6–end Ps. 97 Titus 3. 4–7 Luke 2. [1–7] 8–20 *III* Isa. 52. 7–10 Ps. 98 Heb. 1. 1–4 [5–12] John 1. 1–14	*MP*: Ps. **110**; 117 Isa. 62. 1–5 Matt. 1. 18–end	*EP*: Ps. 8 Isa. 65. 17–25 Phil. 2. 5–11 *or* Luke 2. 1–20 *if it has not been used at the principal service of the day*
26 Tuesday	**STEPHEN, DEACON, FIRST MARTYR**		
R	*The reading from Acts must be used as either the first or second reading at the Eucharist.*	2 Chron. 24. 20–22 *or* Acts 7. 51–end Ps. 119. 161–168 Acts 7. 51–end *or* Gal. 2. 16b–20 Matt. 10. 17–22	*MP*: Ps. **13**; 31. 1–8; 150 Jer. 26. 12–15 Acts ch. 6	*EP*: Ps. 57; **86** Gen. 4. 1–10 Matt. 23. 34–end
27 Wednesday	**JOHN, APOSTLE AND EVANGELIST**		
W		Exod. 33. 7–11a Ps. 117 1 John ch. 1 John 21. 19b–end	*MP*: Ps. **21**; 147. 13–end Exod. 33. 12–end 1 John 2. 1–11	*EP*: Ps. 97 Isa. 6. 1–8 1 John 5. 1–12
28 Thursday	**THE HOLY INNOCENTS**		
R		Jer. 31. 15–17 Ps. 124 1 Cor. 1. 26–29 Matt. 2. 13–18	*MP*: Ps. **36**; 146 Baruch 4. 21–27 *or* Gen. 37. 13–20 Matt. 18. 1–10	*EP*: Ps. 123; **128** Isa. 49. 14–25 Mark 10. 13–16
29 Friday	Thomas Becket, Archbishop of Canterbury, Martyr, 1170*		
Wr	Com. Martyr *or* *esp.* Matt. 10. 28–33 *also* Ecclus. 51. 1–8	1 John 2. 3–11 Ps. 96. 1–4 Luke 2. 22–35	Ps. **19**; 20 Jonah ch. 1 Col. 1. 1–14	Ps. 131; **132** Isa. 57. 15–end John 1. 1–18
30 Saturday			
W		1 John 2. 12–17 Ps. 96. 7–10 Luke 2. 36–40	Ps. 111; 112; **113** Jonah ch. 2 Col. 1. 15–23	Ps. **65**; 84 Isa. 59. 1–15a John 1. 19–28 ct
31 Sunday	**THE FIRST SUNDAY OF CHRISTMAS**		
W		Isa. 61.10 – 62.3 Ps. 148 (*or* 148. 7–end) Gal. 4. 4–7 Luke 2. 15–21	Ps. 105. 1–11 Isa. 63. 7–9 Eph. 3. 5–12	Ps. 132 Isa. ch. 35 Col. 1. 9–20 *or* Luke 2. 41–end

*Thomas Becket may be celebrated on 7 July instead of 29 December.

Calendar and Holy Communion	Morning Prayer	Evening Prayer	NOTES

CHRISTMAS DAY

𝔴	Isa. 9. 2–7 Ps. 98 Heb. 1. 1–12 John 1. 1–14	Ps. 110; 117 Isa. 62. 1–5 Matt. 1. 18–end	Ps. 8 Isa. 65. 17–25 Phil. 2. 5–11 or Luke 2. 1–20

STEPHEN, DEACON, FIRST MARTYR

R	Collect (1) Stephen (2) Christmas 2 Chron. 24. 20–22 Ps. 119. 161–168 Acts 7. 55–end Matt. 23. 34–end	(Ps. 13; 31. 1–8; 150) Jer. 26. 12–15 Acts ch. 6	(Ps. 57; 86) Gen. 4. 1–10 Matt. 10. 17–22

JOHN, APOSTLE AND EVANGELIST

W	Collect (1) John (2) Christmas Exod. 33. 18–end Ps. 92. 11–end 1 John ch. 1 John 21. 19b–end	(Ps. 21; 147. 13–end) Exod. 33. 7–11a 1 John 2. 1–11	(Ps. 97) Isa. 6. 1–8 1 John 5. 1–12

THE HOLY INNOCENTS

R	Collect (1) Innocents (2) Christmas Jer. 31. 10–17 Ps. 123 Rev. 14. 1–5 Matt. 2. 13–18	(Ps. 36; 146) Baruch 4. 21–27 or Gen. 37. 13–20 Matt. 18. 1–10	(Ps. 124; 128) Isa. 49. 14–25 Mark 10. 13–16

W	CEG of Christmas	Jonah ch. 1 Col. 1. 1–14	Isa. 57. 15–end John 1. 1–18

W	CEG of Christmas	Jonah ch. 2 Col. 1. 15–23	Isa. 59. 1–15a John 1. 19–28

ct

THE SUNDAY AFTER CHRISTMAS DAY

W	Isa. 62. 10–12 Ps. 45. 1–7 Gal. 4. 1–7 Matt. 1. 18–end	Ps. 105. 1–11 Isa. 63. 7–9 Eph. 3. 5–12	Ps. 132 Isa. ch. 35 1 John 1. 1–7

The Additional Weekday Lectionary provides two readings on a one-year cycle for each day (except for Sundays, Principal Feasts and Holy Days, Festivals and Holy Week). They 'stand alone' and are intended particularly for use in those churches and cathedrals that attract occasional rather than regular congregations. The Additional Weekday Lectionary has been designed to complement rather than replace the existing Weekday Lectionary. Thus a church with a regular congregation in the morning and a congregation made up mainly of visitors in the evening would continue to use the Weekday Lectionary in the morning but might choose to use this Additional Weekday Lectionary for Evening Prayer.

Psalms are not provided, since the Weekday Lectionary already offers a variety of approaches with regard to psalmody. This Lectionary is not intended for use at the Eucharist; the Daily Eucharistic Lectionary is already authorized for that purpose.

On Sundays, Principal Feasts, other Principal Holy Days, Festivals, and in Holy Week, where no readings are provided in this table, the lectionary provision in the main part of this volume should be used.

Date	Old Testament	New Testament
November 2022		
27 S	THE FIRST SUNDAY OF ADVENT	
28 M	Mal. 3. 1–6	Matt. 3. 1–6
29 Tu	Zeph. 3. 14–end	1 Thess. 4. 13–end
30 W	ANDREW	
December 2022		
1 Th	Mic. 5. 2–5a	John 3. 16–21
2 F	Isa. 66. 18–end	Luke 13. 22–30
3 Sa	Mic. 7. 8–15	Rom. 15.30 – 16.7, 25–end
4 S	THE SECOND SUNDAY OF ADVENT	
5 M	Jer. 7. 1–11	Phil. 4. 4–9
6 Tu	Dan. 7. 9–14	Matt. 24. 15–28
7 W	Amos 9. 11–end	Rom. 13. 8–14
8 Th	Jer. 23. 5–8	Mark 11. 1–11
9 F	Jer. 33. 14–22	Luke 21. 25–36
10 Sa	Zech. 14. 4–11	Rev. 22. 1–7
11 S	THE THIRD SUNDAY OF ADVENT	
12 M	Isa. 40. 1–11	Matt. 3. 1–12
13 Tu	Lam. 3. 22–33	1 Cor. 1. 1–9
14 W	Joel 3. 9–16	Matt. 24. 29–35
15 Th	Isa. ch. 62	1 Thess. 3. 6–13
16 F	Isa. 2. 1–5	Acts 11. 1–18
17 Sa	Ecclus. 224. 1–9 or Prov. 8. 22–31	1 Cor. 2. 1–13
18 S	THE FOURTH SUNDAY OF ADVENT	
19 M	Isa. 11. 1–9	Rom. 15. 7–13
20 Tu	Isa. 22. 21–23	Rev. 3. 7–13
21 W	Num. 24. 15b–19	Rev. 22. 10–21
22 Th	Jer. 30. 7–11a	Acts 4. 1–12
23 F	Isa. 7. 10–15	Matt. 1. 18–23
24 Sa	At Evening Prayer, the readings for Christmas Eve are used. At other services, the following readings are used:	
	Isa. 29. 13–18	1 John 4. 7–16
25 S	**CHRISTMAS DAY**	
26 M	STEPHEN	
27 Tu	JOHN THE EVANGELIST	
28 W	THE HOLY INNOCENTS	
29 Th	Mic. 1. 1–4; 2. 12–13	Luke 2. 1–7
30 F	Isa. 9. 2–7	John 8. 12–20
31 Sa	Eccles. 3. 1–13	Rev. 21. 1–8
January 2023		
1 S	**NAMING AND CIRCUMCISION OF JESUS** (THE SECOND SUNDAY OF CHRISTMAS)	
2 M	Isa. 66. 6–14 or Naming and Circumcision of Jesus	Matt. 12. 46–50
3 Tu	Deut. 6. 4–15	John 10. 31–end
4 W	Isa. 63. 7–16	Gal. 3.23 – 4.7
5 Th	At Evening Prayer, the readings for the Eve of Epiphany are used. At other services, or where, for pastoral reasons, The Epiphany is celebrated on Sunday 8 January, the following readings are used:	
	Isa. ch. 12	2 Cor. 2, 12–end
6 F	**THE EPIPHANY**	

Date	Old Testament	New Testament
	Where, for pastoral reasons, The Epiphany is celebrated on Sunday 8 January, the following readings are used:	
	Gen. 25. 19–end	Eph. 1. 1–6
7 Sa	*Where The Baptism of Christ is celebrated on Sunday 8 January, the readings for the Eve of The Baptism of Christ are used at Evening Prayer. At other services, the following readings are used:*	
	Gen. 25. 19–end	Eph. 1. 1–6
	Where The Epiphany is celebrated on Sunday 8 January, the readings for the Eve of the Epiphany are used at Evening Prayer. At other services, the following readings are used:	
	Joel 2. 28–end	Eph. 1. 7–14
8 S	THE BAPTISM OF CHRIST (The First Sunday of Epiphany)	
9 M	*Where The Epiphany is celebrated on Friday 6 January and the Baptism of Christ on Sunday 8 January, these readings are used on Monday 9 January:*	
	Isa. 41. 14–20	John 1. 29–34
	Where The Epiphany is celebrated on Sunday 8 January, The Baptism of Christ is transferred to Monday 9 January.	
10 Tu	Exod. 17. 1–7	Acts 8. 26–end
11 W	Exod. 15. 1–19	Col. 2. 8–15
12 Th	Zech. 6. 9–15	1 Pet. 2. 4–10
13 F	Isa. 51. 7–16	Gal. 6. 14–18
14 Sa	Lev. 16. 11–22	Heb. 10. 19–25
15 S	THE SECOND SUNDAY OF EPIPHANY	
16 M	1 Kings. 17. 8–16	Mark 8. 1–10
17 Tu	1 Kings 19. 1–9a	Mark 1. 9–15
18 W	1 Kings 19. 9b–18	Mark 9. 2–13
19 Th	Isa. 11. 1–8, 13–19, 41–45	Acts 10. 9–16
20 F	Isa. 49. 8–13	Acts 10. 34–43
21 Sa	Gen. 35. 1–15	Acts 10. 44–end
22 S	THE THIRD SUNDAY OF EPIPHANY	
23 M	Ezek. 37. 15–end	John 17. 1–19
24 Tu	Ezek. 20. 39–44	John 17. 20–end
25 W	THE CONVERSION OF PAUL	
26 Th	Deut. 26. 16–end	Rom. 14. 1–9
27 F	Lev. 19. 9–28	Rom. 15. 1–7
28 Sa	Jer. 33. 1–11	1 Pet. 5. 5b–end
	or, where The Presentation is celebrated on Sunday 29 January, First EP of Presentation of Christ	
29 S	THE FOURTH SUNDAY OF EPIPHANY (or *The Presentation*)	
30 M	Jonah ch. 3	2 Cor. 5. 11–21
31 Tu	Prov. 4. 10–end	Matt. 5. 13–20
February 2023		
1 W	At Evening Prayer, the readings for the Eve of Presentation are used. At other services, the following readings are used:	
	Isa. 61. 1–9	Luke 7. 18–30
2 Th	**THE PRESENTATION** or	
	Isa. 52. 1–12	Matt. 10. 1–15

3	F	Isa. 56. 1–8	Matt. 28. 16–end
4	Sa	Hab. 2. 1–4	Rev. 14. 1–7
5	S	**THE THIRD SUNDAY BEFORE LENT**	
6	M	Exod. 23. 1–13	James 2. 1–13
7	Tu	Deut. 10. 12–end	Heb. 13. 1–16
8	W	Isa. 58. 6–end	Matt. 25. 31–end
9	Th	Isa. 42. 1–9	Luke 4. 14–21
10	F	Amos 5. 6–15	Eph. 4. 25–end
11	Sa	Amos 5. 18–24	John 2. 13–22
12	S	**THE SECOND SUNDAY BEFORE LENT**	
13	M	Isa. 61. 1–9	Mark 6. 1–13
14	Tu	Isa. 52. 1–10	Rom. 10. 5–21
15	W	Isa. 52.13 – 53.6	Rom. 15. 14–21
16	Th	Isa. 53. 4–12	2 Cor. 4. 1–10
17	F	Zech. 8. 16–end	Matt. 10. 1–15
18	Sa	Jer. 1. 4–10	Matt. 10. 16–22
19	S	**THE SUNDAY NEXT BEFORE LENT**	
20	M	2 Kings 2. 13–22	3 John
21	Tu	Judg. 14. 5–17	Rev. 10. 4–11
22	W	**ASH WEDNESDAY**	
23	Th	Gen. 2. 7–end	Heb. 2. 5–end
24	F	Gen. 4. 1–12	Heb. 4. 12–end
25	Sa	2 Kings 22. 11–end	Heb. 5. 1–10
26	S	**THE FIRST SUNDAY OF LENT**	
27	M	Gen. 6. 11–end; 7. 11–16	Luke 4. 14–21
28	Tu	Deut. 31. 7–13	1 John 3. 1–10

March 2023

1	W	Gen. 11. 1–9	Matt. 24. 15–28
2	Th	Gen. 13. 1–13	1 Pet. 2. 13–end
3	F	Gen. 21. 1–8	Luke 9. 18–27
4	Sa	Gen. 32. 22–32	2 Pet. 1. 10–end
5	S	**THE SECOND SUNDAY OF LENT**	
6	M	1 Chron. 21. 1–17	1 John 2. 1–8
7	Tu	Zech. ch. 3	2 Pet. 2. 1–10a
8	W	Job. 1. 1–22	Luke 21.34 – 22.6
9	Th	2 Chron. 29. 1–11	Mark 11. 15–19
10	F	Exod. 19. 1–9a	1 Pet. 1. 1–9
11	Sa	Exod. 19. 9b–19	Acts 7. 44–50
12	S	**THE THIRD SUNDAY OF LENT**	
13	M	Josh. 4. 1–13	Luke 9. 1–11
14	Tu	Exod. 15. 2–27	Heb. 10. 32–end
15	W	Gen. 9. 8–17	1 Pet. 3. 18–end
16	Th	Dan. 12. 5–end	Mark 13. 21–end
17	F	Num. 20. 1–13	1 Cor. 10. 23–end
18	Sa	Isa. 43. 14–end	Heb. 3. 1–15
19	S	**THE FOURTH SUNDAY OF LENT (Mothering Sunday)**	
20	M	**JOSEPH OF NAZARETH** (transferred)	
21	Tu	Jer. 13. 12–19	Acts 13. 26–35
22	W	Jer. 13. 20–27	1 Pet. 1.17 – 2.3
23	Th	Jer. 22. 11–19	Luke 11. 37–52
24	F	*At Evening Prayer, the readings for the Eve of the Annunciation are used. At other services, the following readings are used:* Jer. 17. 1–14	Luke 6. 17–26
25	Sa	**THE ANNUNCIATION**	
26	S	**THE FIFTH SUNDAY OF LENT (Passiontide begins)**	
27	M	Joel 2. 12–17	2 John
28	Tu	Isa. 58. 1–14	Mark 10. 32–45
29	W	Joel 36. 1–12	John 14. 1–14
30	Th	Jer. 9. 17–22	Luke 13. 31–35
31	F	Lam. 5. 1–3, 19–22	John 12. 20–26

April 2023

1	Sa	Job 17. 6–end	John 12. 27–36
2	S	**PALM SUNDAY** HOLY WEEK	
9	S	**EASTER DAY**	
10	M	Isa. 54. 1–14	Rom. 1. 1–7
11	Tu	Isa. 51. 1–11	John 5. 19–29
12	W	Isa. 26. 1–19	John 20. 1–10
13	Th	Isa. 43. 14–21	Rev. 1. 4–end
14	F	Isa. 42. 10–17	1 Thess. 5. 1–11
15	Sa	Job 14. 1–14	John 21. 1–14
16	S	**THE SECOND SUNDAY OF EASTER**	
17	M	Ezek. 1. 22–end	Rev. ch. 4
18	Tu	Prov. 8. 1–11	Acts 16. 6–15
19	W	Hos. 5.15 – 6.6	1 Cor. 15. 1–11
20	Th	Jonah ch. 2	Mark 4. 35–end
21	F	Gen. 6. 9–end	1 Pet. 3. 8–end
22	Sa	1 Sam. 2. 1–8	Matt. 28. 8–15
23	S	**THE THIRD SUNDAY OF EASTER**	
24	M	**GEORGE** (transferred)	
25	Tu	**MARK**	
26	W	Gen. 3. 8–21	1 Cor. 15. 12–28
27	Th	Isa. 33. 13–22	Mark 6. 47–end
28	F	Neh. 9. 6–17	Rom. 5. 12–end
29	Sa	Isa. 61.10 – 62.5	Luke 24. 1–12
30	S	**THE FOURTH SUNDAY OF EASTER**	

May 2023

1	M	**PHILIP AND JAMES**	
2	Tu	Job 31. 13–23	Matt. 7. 1–12
3	W	Gen. 2. 4b–9	1 Cor. 15. 35–49
4	Th	Prov. 28. 3–end	Mark 10. 17–31
5	F	Eccles. 12. 1–8	Rom. 6. 1–11
6	Sa	1 Chron. 29. 10–13	Luke 24. 13–35
7	S	**THE FIFTH SUNDAY OF EASTER**	
8	M	Gen. 15. 1–18	Rom. 4. 13–end
9	Tu	Deut. 8. 1–10	Matt. 6. 19–end
10	W	Hos. 13. 4–14	1 Cor. 15. 50–end
11	Th	Exod. 3. 1–15	Mark 12. 18–27
12	F	Ezek. 36. 33–end	Rom. 8. 1–11
13	Sa	Isa. 38. 9–20	Luke 24. 33–end
14	S	**THE SIXTH SUNDAY OF EASTER**	
15	M	**MATTHIAS** (transferred from 14 May) *Where Matthias is celebrated on 24 February:* Prov. 4. 1–13	Phil. 2. 1–11
16	Tu	Isa. 32. 12–end	Rom. 5. 1–11
17	W	*At Evening Prayer, the readings for the Eve of Ascension Day are used. At other services, the following readings are used:* Isa. 43. 1–13	Titus 2.11 – 3.8
18	Th	**ASCENSION DAY**	
19	F	Exod. 35.30 – 36.1	Gal. 5. 13–end
20	Sa	Num. 11. 16–17, 24–29	1 Cor. ch. 2
21	S	**THE SEVENTH SUNDAY OF EASTER** (Sunday after Ascension Day)	
22	M	Num. 27. 15–end	1 Cor. ch. 3
23	Tu	1 Sam. 10. 1–10	1 Cor. 12. 1–13
24	W	1 Kings 19. 1–18	Matt. 3. 13–end
25	Th	Ezek. 11. 14–20	Matt. 9.35 – 10.20
26	F	Ezek. 36. 22–28	Matt. 12. 22–32
27	Sa	*At Evening Prayer, the readings for the Eve of Pentecost are used. At other services, the following readings are used:* Mic. 3. 1–8	Eph. 6. 10–20
28	S	**PENTECOST** (Whit Sunday)	
29	M	Gen. 12. 1–9	Rom. 4. 13–end
30	Tu	Gen. 13. 1–12	Rom. 12. 9–end
31	W	**THE VISITATION** *Where The Visitation is celebrated on 2 July:* Gen. ch. 15	Rom. 4. 1–8

June 2023

1	Th	Gen. 22. 1–18	Heb. 11. 8–19
2	F	Isa. 51. 1–8	John 8. 48–end
3	Sa	*At Evening Prayer, the readings for the Eve of Trinity Sunday are used. At other services, the following readings are used:* Ecclus. 44. 19–23 *or* Josh. 2. 1–15	James 2. 14–26
4	S	**TRINITY SUNDAY**	
5	M	Exod. 2. 1–10	Heb. 11. 23–31
6	Tu	Exod. 2. 11–end	Acts 7. 17–29
7	W	Exod. 3. 1–12	Acts 7. 30–38

8	S	THE EIGHTEENTH SUNDAY AFTER TRINITY	
9	M	2 Sam. 22. 4–7, 17–20	Heb. 7.26 – 8.6
10	Tu	Prov. 22. 17–end	2 Cor. 12. 1–10
11	W	Hos. ch. 14	James 2. 14–26
12	Th	Isa. 24. 1–15	John 16. 25–33
13	F	Jer. 14. 1–9	Luke 23. 44–56
14	Sa	Zech. 8. 14–end	John 20. 19–end
15	S	THE NINETEENTH SUNDAY AFTER TRINITY	
16	M	1 Kings 3. 3–14	1 Tim. 3.13 – 4.8
17	Tu	Prov. 27. 11–end	Gal. 6. 1–10
18	W	LUKE	
19	Th	Ecclus. 18. 1–14	1 Cor. 11. 17–end
		or Job ch. 26	
20	F	Ecclus. 28. 2–12	Mark 15. 33–37
		or Job 19. 21–end	
21	Sa	Isa. 44. 21–end	John 21. 15–end
22	S	THE TWENTIETH SUNDAY AFTER TRINITY	
23	M	1 Kings 6. 2–10	John 12. 1–11
24	Tu	Prov. 31. 10–end	Luke 10. 38–42
25	W	Jonah ch. 1	Luke 5. 1–11
26	Th	Exod. 12. 1–20	1 Thess. 4. 1–12
27	F	Isa. ch. 64	Matt. 27. 45–56
28	Sa	SIMON AND JUDE	
29	S	THE LAST SUNDAY AFTER TRINITY	
30	M	Isa. 42. 14–21	Luke 1. 5–25
31	Tu	At Evening Prayer, the readings for the Eve of All Saints are used. At other services, the following readings are used:	
		1 Sam. 4. 12–end	Luke 1. 57–80

November 2023

1	W	ALL SAINTS' DAY	
		or, where All Saints' Day is celebrated on Sunday 5 November:	
		Baruch ch. 5	Mark 1. 1–11
		or Hagg. 1. 1–11	
2	Th	Isa. ch. 35	Matt. 11. 2–19
3	F	2 Sam. 11. 1–17	Matt. 14. 1–12
4	Sa	Isa. 43. 15–21	Acts 19. 1–10
5	S	THE FOURTH SUNDAY BEFORE ADVENT	
6	M	Esth. 3. 1–11; 4. 7–17	Matt. 18. 1–10
7	Tu	Ezek. 18. 21–end	Matt. 18. 12–20
8	W	Prov. 3. 27–end	Matt. 18. 21–end
9	Th	Exod. 23. 1–9	Matt. 19. 1–15
10	F	Prov. 3. 13–18	Matt. 19. 16–end
11	Sa	Deut. 28. 1–6	Matt. 20. 1–16
12	S	THE THIRD SUNDAY BEFORE ADVENT	
13	M	Isa. 40. 21–end	Rom. 11. 25–end
14	Tu	Ezek. 34. 20–end	John 10. 1–18
15	W	Lev. 26. 3–13	Titus 2. 1–10
16	Th	Hos. 6. 1–6	Matt. 9. 9–13
17	F	Mal. ch. 4	John 4. 5–26

18	Sa	Mic. 6. 6–8	Col. 3. 12–17
19	S	THE SECOND SUNDAY BEFORE ADVENT	
20	M	Mic. 7. 1–7	Matt. 10. 24–39
21	Tu	Hab. 3. 1–19a	1 Cor. 4. 9–16
22	W	Zech. 8. 1–13	Mark 13. 3–8
23	Th	Zech. 10. 6–end	1 Pet. 5. 1–11
24	F	Mic. 4. 1–5	Luke 9. 28–36
25	Sa	At Evening Prayer, the readings for the Eve of Christ the King are used. At other services, the following readings are used:	
		Exod. 16. 1–21	John 6. 3–15
26	S	CHRIST THE KING (The Sunday next before Advent)	
27	M	Jer. 30. 1–3, 10–17	Rom. 12. 9–21
28	Tu	Jer. 30. 18–24	John 10. 22–30
29	W	Jer. 31. 1–9	Matt. 15. 21–31
30	Th	ANDREW	

December 2023

1	F	Jer. 31. 31–37	Heb. 10. 11–18
2	Sa	Isa. 51.17 – 52.2	Eph. 5. 1–20
3	S	THE FIRST SUNDAY OF ADVENT	
4	M	Mal. 3. 1–6	Matt. 3. 1–6
5	Tu	Zeph. 3. 14–end	1 Thess. 4. 13–end
6	W	Isa. 65.17 – 66.2	Matt. 24. 1–14
7	Th	Mic. 5. 2–5a	John 3. 16–21
8	F	Isa. 66. 18–end	Luke 13. 22–30
9	Sa	Mic. 7. 8–15	Rom. 15.30 – 16.7, 25–end
10	S	THE SECOND SUNDAY OF ADVENT	
11	M	Jer. 7. 1–11	Phil. 4. 4–9
12	Tu	Dan. 7. 9–14	Matt. 24. 15–28
13	W	Amos 9. 11–end	Rom. 13. 8–14
14	Th	Jer. 23. 5–8	Mark 11. 1–11
15	F	Jer. 33. 14–22	Luke 21. 25–36
16	Sa	Zech. 14. 4–11	Rev. 22. 1–7
17	S	THE THIRD SUNDAY OF ADVENT	
18	M	Jer. 3. 1–6	Acts 7. 20–36
19	Tu	Isa. 11. 1–9	Rom. 15. 7–13
20	W	Isa. 22. 21–23	Rev. 3. 7–13
21	Th	Num. 24. 15b–19	Rev. 22. 10–21
22	F	Jer. 30. 7–11a	Acts 4. 1–12
23	Sa	Isa. 7. 10–15	Matt. 1. 18–23
24	S	THE FOURTH SUNDAY OF ADVENT (Christmas Eve)	
25	M	CHRISTMAS DAY	
26	Tu	STEPHEN	
27	W	JOHN THE EVANGELIST	
28	Th	THE HOLY INNOCENTS	
29	F	Mic. 1. 1–4; 2. 12–13	Luke 2. 1–7
30	Sa	Isa. 9. 2–7	John 8. 12–20
31	S	THE FIRST SUNDAY OF CHRISTMAS	

CALENDAR 2023

JANUARY
Su	M	Tu	W	Th	F	Sa
X¹	:	:	:	:	:	E³
2	B	E¹	E²	E²⁰	E⁴	:
3	9	16	17	24	31	:
Tu	10	17	24	31	:	:
W	11	18	25	:	:	:
Th	12	19	26	:	:	:
F	13	20	27	:	:	:
Sa	14	21	28	:	:	:

FEBRUARY
LL³ L⁻² L⁻¹ L

MARCH
L² L³ L⁴ L⁵

APRIL
MAY
JUNE
JULY
AUGUST
SEPTEMBER
OCTOBER
NOVEMBER
DECEMBER

Key:
- A = Ash Wednesday, Ascension, Advent
- A⁻ = Before Advent
- A⁻¹ = also All Saints, 2023 and 2024 (if transferred)
- A⁻² = Christ the King
- An = Annunciation
- AS = All Saints
- B = Baptism
- E = Epiphany, Easter
- E¹ = also Presentation, 2023 and 2024 (if transferred)
- G = Good Friday
- L = Lent
- L⁻ = Before Lent

- M = Maundy Thursday
- P = Palm Sunday
- Pr = Presentation
- T = Trinity

CALENDAR 2024

JANUARY
FEBRUARY
MARCH
APRIL
MAY
JUNE
JULY
AUGUST
SEPTEMBER
OCTOBER
NOVEMBER
DECEMBER

Key:
- (T¹ = also Barnabas, 2023)
- (T⁴ = also Transfiguration, 2023)
- (T¹⁸ = also Michael and All Angels, 2024)

- T⁻ = Last Sunday after Trinity
- W = Pentecost (Whit Sunday)
- X = Christmas